Travis McGee & Me

Reflections on the Man from Slip F-18

D. R. Martin

Conger Road Press
Minneapolis, Minnesota

Copyright © 2014 D. R. Martin

Published by Conger Road Press
Minneapolis, Minnesota

All rights reserved. No part of this book may be reproduced in whole or in part, scanned, photocopied, recorded, distributed in any printed or electronic form, or reproduced in any manner whatsoever, or by any information storage and retrieval system now known or hereafter invented, without written permission of the author, except in the case of brief quotations embodied in critical or journalistic articles and reviews.

All rights reserved.
Cover Photograph © 1995 D.R. Martin
Cover Design © 2014 D.R. Martin

ISBN-13: 978-0-9850196-7-9

Introduction: Say Hello to Travis McGee

By the time he published his first Travis McGee adventure in 1964, John D. MacDonald (JDM) had written dozens of novels and scores of short stories. He populated them with relatively ordinary people who found themselves caught in terrible binds—ensnared by their own weaknesses or the traps that others set for them. Sex, power, greed, corruption, venality, egotism, hatred, heroism, selflessness, stupidity, nobility, and evil itself course powerfully through JDM's tales. Just as Georges Simenon, creator of the peerless Maigret series, understood what was ticking away beneath the carapace of the human skull, so did JDM. In fact, I would cast JDM—with his deep insight into the psychology of people under extreme pressure—as America's own Simenon.

So when Fawcett Books came to JDM in the early 1960s with the proposal to create a series based on a tough-guy, PI-type character, he was ready to go. He had tested several McGee-like protagonists in earlier novels and wasn't about to mimic the glib tough guys of less capable writers (e.g., the likes of Brett Halliday and

Richard Prather, whom he replaced in the Fawcett stable). Nor did he copy those inscrutable literary shamuses Sam Spade (Dashiel Hammett), Philip Marlowe (Raymond Chandler), and Lew Archer (Ross MacDonald). Travis McGee was about to raise the bar on crime fiction to its highest level ever. JDM's twenty-one McGee stories would go beyond anything the hard-boiled-fiction world had seen before, and serve as the template for the best detective/PI series of the 1970s and beyond—such as Spenser and V. I. Warshawski, Elvis Cole and Doc Ford. (Not that any of those aspirants ever lived up to the boat bum from Ft. Lauderdale, in my opinion.)

With philosopher/knight-errant McGee, every case was personal. Whether he sortied out from the *Busted Flush* (his houseboat home) to defend or avenge a friend, or to undertake a salvage project for his fifty percent cut, he brought with him his sense of justice. Righting the balance of things was always important to McGee.

For someone who perennially poked his nose into dangerous places, he had the complete toolkit. Crafty, muscular fighting skills. A sort of rough-hewn charm and sexiness. Sharp instincts and reflexes. An intellect capable of untangling thorny problems. A sound understanding of human psychology. The classic hard-boiled PI conscience. The deceptiveness of a good con man. Knowledge of the ways of commerce and politics. And an ability to recruit good people to the cause.

Above all, McGee brought a questing personal outlook. More insistently than almost any other protagonist in mystery and suspense, he shared his thoughts on the ways that the world was going—typically, to hell in a handbasket. (McGee died in 1986 with his creator, and I think he would be amazed that we aren't more screwed up than we are at this point.)

His ruminations on love, mortality, and the fate of American society are some of the most heartfelt and insightful in all of genre fiction. Decades before most of us were aware of them, McGee reflected on our potential for environmental disaster and the inevitability of terrorism. He laid it all out for us, and spoke it as he saw it, sometimes at excessive length. His twenty-one adventures constitute one of the under-appreciated treasures of twentieth-century American literature.

Anyone, though, who samples McGee needs to keep in mind that these tales are now period pieces. Though McGee treated women with far greater respect than many of his fictional predecessors, the stories are not politically correct in terms of today's outlooks on gender issues. Many who've tried these books can't stand McGee's POV on women. He is a man of his era, after all, with everything that entails.

Travis McGee & Me is my book-by-book personal take on a character and a writer who have become very important to me, ever since a mystery-writing teacher put me onto McGee nearly twenty-five years ago. Every summer I've read four or five McGees, usually in my backyard, sitting under the shade of a very old, very large elm. And however many times I've read *Blue* or

Gray or *Scarlet*, I always treasure my time hanging with Travis and (in middle and later books) his sidekick Meyer. These essays are partly book reports, and partly my opinions on the best and worst of McGee. They originally appeared in my blog, which is still active at http://drmar120.wordpress.com/.

All twenty-one McGee books have been in print continuously ever since their original publications, and have lately reappeared in new trade paperback editions, as e-books, and as audio books. A major movie based on *The Deep Blue Good-by* was to have been filmed in 2015, starring Christian Bale. But the actor sustained a knee injury prior to production and filming had to be postponed. No word yet when the film will start up again.

You can get the books new almost anywhere. And because tens of millions of JDM paperbacks have adorned book-racks since the 1950s, the McGees and his forty other novels are often available in used bookstores and online at minimal cost. I found many of mine for a buck each, some for as low as 25 cents.

Do you need to begin at the beginning, with 1964's *The Deep Blue Good-by*? I didn't, the first time through. But if you're methodical about such things, maybe it's a good idea. I think it's safe to say that if *Blue* strikes a chord with you, you'll like what follows.

Otherwise, my advice is to just pick a color—all McGee titles feature colors—from the early or middle books. That would include *Blue, Pink, Purple, Red, Gold, Orange, Amber, Yellow, Gray, Brown, Indigo, Lavender, Tan,* or *Scarlet*. (My particular favorites in that group are *Blue*, *Gray*, and *Lavender*.) Then sit back and be transported to the heart of the 1960s, to Slip F-18, Bahia Mar, Ft. Lauderdale, Florida.

D. R. Martin
Minneapolis, Minnesota

1. The Deep Blue Good-by

The first time anyone encounters Travis McGee, he is ensconced in the *Busted Flush*, the ponderous old houseboat that he won in a poker game and moors in Slip F-18, Bahia Mar, Ft. Lauderdale. As he lounges, a lithe but athletic young lady is improbably working on her choreography in his "living room." And just as improbably, that young lady sets Travis off on his first recorded adventure.

It seems that one of her dancers, Cathy, was due a kind of shady inheritance from her dead dad, some loot he stole in his army days. Problem is, Dad's former cellmate—a scary, grinning fellow name of Junior Allen—came to "help" the widow and daughters, and found the hidden loot first. Would Travis consider giving the young lady a hand to get some of it back? Travis lives the American dream by working only when he needs to; living off his slush fund when he can. But when presented this opportunity to don the decrepit armor, climb back up on that old swaybacked nag, and charge into the breech... Well he can't resist.

It's important to note that Travis is not a PI, not a

shamus. He often goes sleuthing in his twenty-one adventures. But what he does primarily is "recover" things that people have lost or had taken from them, things that are not recoverable by ordinary legal means—money, treasure, reputation. If something has monetary value, he takes 50 percent of the recovery. When he has enough money tucked away, he enjoys his retirement in installments. When he runs low, he goes back to work. In many of the stories, he ends up working pro bono—as he does in *The Deep Blue Good-By* (1964). Sometimes the only recovery is retribution, for friends who have been murdered (see *Gray* and *Green*).

Once mounted on his "spavined steed," figuratively speaking, Travis heads to the small town in the Florida Keys where Junior Allen romanced Cathy and stole the inheritance out from under her. Amazingly, Allen, jingling with money, has had the chutzpah to come back in a fancy, big cabin cruiser. He takes possession of an attractive divorcee named Lois Atkinson. He sexually uses her, abuses her, degrades her, and abandons her, leaving her emotionally ruined. Travis—in his first restoration of a shattered female—brings Lois slowly and delicately back among the living. And, with a little help from the lady, he goes after the monster, playing Beowulf to Junior's Grendel.

Travis's first order of business is to find out just what kind of treasure Junior Allen pried out of its hideyhole on the property of Cathy's family. The trail leads him to a bluff, hearty Texas businessman who was a member of the dead father's WWII aircrew and apparently part of the shady dealings. Here Travis commits his first big moral and legal transgression. When the hearty businessman stonewalls him, Travis knocks him cold, hauls him off to a motel room, strips him, ties him up, dumps him in the shower, and scalds him with hot water. The businessman quickly tells how Cathy's dad and his aircrew ran a smuggling operation during the war, converting their booty into gemstones that could be easily gotten back into the U.S. Travis at least has the decency to not enjoy this "interrogation," but it's not nice, not nice at all. This is torture, pure and simple.

Travis tracks down Junior Allen and sets up a sting that's going to relieve the grinning man of his treasure. But Lois begs Travis not to do it. Have the police arrest Junior instead. She and Cathy (who set the adventure in motion and was beaten up by Junior earlier in the story) will testify against him for kidnapping, rape, and assault. Junior will go down for a good many years. Travis, wanting to punish Junior in his own way and wanting to get at that treasure, says no and initiates his plan. Things go sour in a hurry, as Travis gets his lights punched out on Junior's boat. When he wakes up, he manages to rescue Junior's next intended victim, a pretty teenager, and swim ashore. That's where he finds out that Lois had come looking for him and was taken by Junior. Travis mounts a one-man rescue operation, slays the monster, and finds Lois below deck, beaten within an inch of her life—which ends a few days later.

Of course, it's hard to imagine that Lois is stupid enough to walk up to Junior's cruiser, even if she has become Travis's lover—in a tentative, iffy sort of way. (Neither of them seems sure that their brief affair is the best thing.) After all, this is a woman who was begging Travis to let the cops corral Junior Allen. Yet JDM forces her to face the grinning monster one last time.

Junior Allen may have executed Lois Atkinson, but Travis condemned her—inadvertently, stupidly—because his determination to punish Junior and get the treasure back is so overpowering. Travis doesn't explicitly address the fact that this unnecessary sacrifice was as much his doing as Junior Allen's. But I think he knows.

I believe JDM took this option because it's necessary for Travis to not merely be a hero, but a very flawed and morally ambiguous hero. This is how Travis goes beyond the run-of-the-mill, two-dimensional tough guy of 1960s paperback racks. He may be a character who always comes out on top—the guy you want on your side in a fight—but he takes moral and physical damage doing it. Think of an exhausted, battered soldier slogging off the battlefield, buddies dead in the mud behind him. Win or lose, this is no happy camper. He can feel the wear and tear.

Not just a few Grendels are slain in these twenty-one suspenseful morality tales. So too are good people who happen to be Travis's allies. The series reveals the high cost of heroism to the hero and his circle. It's a dangerous thing being close to Travis McGee.

2. Nightmare in Pink

Nightmare, indeed.

Of all the dark places that Travis McGee went to in his twenty-one adventures, there are few darker or grimmer than in this descent into madness and despair.

McGee begins *Nightmare in Pink* (1964) by doing a big favor for an old army buddy who's blind, crippled from his war wounds, and not likely to live much longer. It seems this friend has a little sister whose fiancé has been murdered under suspicious circumstances. Would Travis check things out, and make sure the kid's safe? Shake her up, if you need to, he tells McGee.

Travis leaves the *Busted Flush* behind and heads north to Manhattan. The young man Nina Gibson was going to marry had worked in a real estate investment firm owned by an old-money businessman called Charles Armister. The future husband believed that financial shenanigans were going on at the company, which had been selling properties for a year or two—millions of dollars worth of properties. The young man was subsequently murdered in an apparent street mugging, but Nina doesn't believe that's why he was killed. Travis restrains himself briefly—feeling guilty about betraying his ol' army buddy Mike—but soon is bedding the young lady.

With the help of a wealthy friend, Travis connects with Charlie Armister's sister-in-law. Charlie, it seems, has gone off the rails—left his wife, isolated himself, and become quite the randy, unrepressed personality after a lifetime of stodginess. She suggests ways for Travis to get closer to the situation. He cases the Armister digs and makes a run at the executive assistant. Upping the ante, he tries to penetrate the Armister operation by getting close to a high-end hooker who was known to service the newly horny Mr. Armister. As our blundering hero later observes, he's in way over his head—like a mouse capering with a cobra.

The cobra's bite isn't merely a Mickey slipped to McGee by the high-end hooker. It's far nastier, a powerful hallucinogenic that makes him go crazy in a very public place. He ends up in a mental institution operated by a medical researcher bought and paid for by Charlie's attorney, Baynard Mulligan.

For McGee, it's the mother of all nightmares—an unknowable period of constant drugging and dreadful, disgusting hallucinations that resemble nothing so much as the darkest and foulest of LSD trips. When Travis's insulted mind is allowed to bubble up into a semblance of rationality, Mulligan appears before him to gloat about his scheme to plunder the Armister millions. The whole plan revolved around rendering Charlie Armister as pliable as possible. So the millionaire was drugged, deposited in the asylum, and—a true horror—lobotomized. Thus neutered, the now slow-witted, happy Charlie was easily convinced to leave his wife and family. He became roomies with Mulligan, started bonking the chicks, signed legal documents unwittingly, and neglected to notice the plundering of his fortune. Nina's fiancé was headed for the same fate, but ironically was murdered in an actual botched mugging. Mulligan would never have been so ham-handed as to kill the man outright. He has similar plans for Travis—a little cut of the gray matter and say hi to the life of a good-natured dimwit working in a Jersey shoe factory.

Things are looking very bad indeed, when JDM works up a simple *deus ex machina*: Someone forgets to give Travis his dose, and the rangy boat bum bubbles up again into something like rationality. He manages to get loose, kills an attendant, and then purloins a few vials of the head-warping drug and dumps them in the cafeteria coffee machine. Things go to hell at the asylum in a big hurry, with four people dying and dozens of others damaged by the hallucinogenic. Readers would assume they weren't all part of the conspiracy. (As I observed in my notes on *The Deep Blue Good-by*, people who come within Travis's sphere of influence can get hurt or killed. It's not a nice place to be.) Needless to say, Mulligan's plot is effectively shut down.

Ultimately Travis—still suffering from effects of the

drug—learns from authorities that the baddies have all had their comeuppances. Travis pockets a nice check from Mrs. Armister—happy to have her transformed husband back. Sadly, Nina's brother—McGee's buddy—dies after surgery. After the funeral, McGee brings the sister down to the *Flush* for some of that old McGee therapy. After a brief idyll—each restoring the other—the boat bum and the kid sister say farewell.

When I first read *Pink* many years ago, I felt that it was a dreadful kind of fever dream—for a time my least favorite McGee. I think what disappointed me about it was its lack of a humid Florida setting (McGee's natural habitat)…its glowering, dark depiction of a 1960s Manhattan that doesn't jibe with my image of the place…a truly grim, nauseating modus operandi for the villain of the piece…a maladroit, unmasterful McGee who is little more than a bull in a china shop (or mouse in a cobra pit).

I can tolerate *Pink* more easily now. Why? Because JDM—more so than with *Blue*—is telling us that McGee isn't going to be your typical fictional tough guy/hero ("typical" for the preceding era, at any rate). He's going to be flawed and clumsy. He wins in the end and dispenses with the villains, but there is often collateral damage. The boat bum is a very imperfect protagonist for a harsh modern world that was taking shape within a year of JFK's murder. McGee is a new creature in genre fiction, and you'd better get used to him.

3. A Purple Place for Dying

A Purple Place for Dying is the last tale in JDM's original Travis McGee trilogy—three game-changing crime novels that came out in May and June of 1964. While the debut volume (*Blue*) is a vivid, visceral annunciation of a very different kind of hero and the second (*Pink*) a queasy but memorable anomaly, *Purple* shows JDM settling down, beginning to ride the groove that would propel him through two-plus decades of McGee. Pretty much a straight-ahead murder mystery, *Purple* features a McGee who's more comfortable in his skin and in his voice, and who presides over a brisk, propulsive, and enjoyable adventure.

Once again, McGee is lured away from Florida. But this time he doesn't do a favor for a friend—as in the first two books. He's considering a prospective job. Buxom, blonde Mona Yeoman is sure that her wealthy old husband has plundered the trust fund her father set up for her. And she wants McGee—the salvage expert—to help her get some of it back. She's in love with a young college professor and that money could finance their escape. McGee has flown out west to meet with her, on her dime. He's inclined to say "No thanks" and head home. But something happens that convinces him to stick around.

He and Mona are standing at the edge of a cliff outside her cabin—in Arizona, unless I miss my guess—just talking. He hears something like an ax striking meat. Mona collapses, instantly dead. Then comes the report of a sniper's rifle, from somewhere off in the distance. McGee evades the sniper, gets to a dusty diner on a desert road, and summons help. When he and the sheriff get back to the cabin, Mona's body has vanished, the cliff edge swept clean. And McGee is pegged as part of a plot to help the happy couple make their getaway. In fact, a pair meeting the general description of Mona and her boyfriend flew out of a nearby airport at about the right time. No one believes Travis when he declares that Mona Yeoman was murdered.

The professor/boyfriend's sister doesn't believe it, until she accompanies McGee to that airport to recover her brother's abandoned car. McGee talks to a stewardess who saw that couple on their flight, and he determines that they couldn't have been the real missing couple. Then the police report comes in: A speck of lung tissue was found at the cliff edge, matching Mona's blood type. The conspiracy actually happened and it was murder, cold-blooded and carefully planned. And though it might make sense to head back to Slip F-18, McGee's dander is up.

The Lauderdale beach bum makes an alliance of mutual interest with Mona's husband, Jass Yeoman. Jass is one of those proverbial big frogs in a small pond—a longtime shaker and mover in the desert community. In the old days, he and Mona's daddy had been best friends, womanizers, and hell raisers, as they built their business empires. (It is said that Jass sired scads of half-Mexican babies all over the countryside.) When Mona's daddy died, Jass became her guardian. He claims he married her when she had grown up because they properly fell in love. He admits that he did plunder Mona's trust fund to save his own financial skin. In fact, the IRS is building a big case against him.

Safely in Jass's employ—and thus free from the sheriff's jail threats for illegal detecting—Travis sallies forth after the killer(s). Along the way he finds and fingers the fake Mona from the airport…interviews Mona's Mexican maidservant…kills a knife-wielding assassin trying to eviscerate Jass…learns about the discovery of the professor's body…saves the sister from suicide. He arranges to meet Jass again, but the new widower has something else keeping him busy: a gruesome dance of death by strychnine. Not least, McGee and the professor's sister have a nearly fatal interlude in a "purple place for dying."

Since this is a pure whodunit, rather than a recovery or revenge story, I'll say no more. No reason to spoil your fun. But I will say that JDM has concocted a solid little thriller with some nice twists and turns. *Purple* is also notable for containing the first mention of McGee's future sidekick, counselor, and best friend, the semi-retired economist with but a single name—Meyer.

4. The Quick Red Fox

The Quick Red Fox (1964) takes the intrepid boat bum and tarnished white knight from one coast to another, and points in between. Florida, upstate New York, California, Vegas, Arizona. Think of it as a mid-1960s picaresque of sex, blackmail, and violence.

McGee's fourth adventure starts off as a straight recovery job. It seems that the eponymous fox—the exquisite, sexy movie star Lysa Dean—has gotten herself comprehensively photographed while participating in a multi-day, alfresco orgy somewhere in Big Sur. The actress paid the first round of blackmail and thought herself free of danger. Now a second series of demands has arrived and she needs to put a lid on it—or her impending marriage to a very wealthy but straight-laced fellow could go bye-bye. She's tracked down McGee through an old mutual friend and sent her very capable aide Dana Holtzer to hire him. Travis's assignment is to stop the blackmail and get back as much of her money as possible. But with Mrs. Holtzer in tow.

At first Dana is a bit of a cold fish, but she has good

reason. Her son is institutionalized. Her epileptic husband was shot by a panicked policeman and is in a vegetative state. She and McGee are a bit prickly with each other at the outset. But they work up a routine of playing a fictional suburban couple who affectionately snipe at one another. Over the course of the story, one thing leads to another and what had been a purely official relationship becomes—surprise, surprise—very much closer. Travis shows signs of falling hard for the lady, but, alas, something unpleasant befalls Dana in the home stretch. She doesn't die, but her fondness for McGee does.

McGee and Dana begin their investigation by tracking down the fox's fellow orgy participants. First on their docket is the deranged, nymphomaniac daughter of a famous architect. The girl is safely ensconced in a Florida facility for drunks and druggies. Then it's on to the leonine ski pro with the fake German accent, busily impressing the chickies at a third-rate resort up in New York. McGee cuts him from his pack of admirers with the lie that Lysa Dean herself is waiting nearby—wanting more of what he provided in Big Sur. Believing speed is of the essence, Travis wallops the ersatz Kraut and threatens to kill him if he doesn't spill everything he knows about the alfresco orgy. Travis, as usual, is unhappy about ambushing and torturing, but the ends justify the means. Dana wonders why he does such things. He says maybe he likes it, and that makes him uncomfortable.

The trail next leads to the drunk girl's brother, who had put her in the custody of an ocean-yachting couple also present at the orgy—the M'Gruders, since divorced. Travis and Dana figure out the identity of the photographer who shot the infamous outdoor party, himself recently murdered. But someone's still blackmailing Lysa Dean. The clues eventually take Travis and Dana to Vegas, to debrief the former Mrs. M'Gruder—who also has just gotten herself murdered. Someone is brutally, desperately brushing the trail clean, one murder at a time. Like a huge, multi-colored neon arrow in the desert, all signs point inexorably toward Mr. M'Gruder, about to marry the girl of his dreams.

And that's as much as I'll say. Because in *Quick Red Fox*, JDM uncorks one of the niftiest curves in all twenty-one McGee adventures. It had been several years since I'd read the book, and happily I had forgotten JDM's bit of legerdemain. (Don't you love it when you forget the good twists in books you're re-reading?) I went for it hook, line, and sinker. When that zinger comes at you out of left field, you're thinking, *Holy cow!* JDM's bombshell practically gives me goose bumps. Again!

For those who are working through the McGee books, all the way from *Blue* to *Silver*, it's worth noting that *Red* is not Lysa Dean's only appearance. Recently I'd been thinking that the fate JDM reserved for the Hollywood diva, in her ultimate McGee adventure (*Freefall in Crimson*), was unreasonably cruel. But when she met with McGee to settle accounts at the end of

Red—and tried to substitute a roll in the satin sheets for some of the money she owed, to treat him like a rube—I was reminded that she at least partially deserved what she ultimately got.

5. A Deadly Shade of Gold

This 1965 paperback original is the most expansive and byzantine tale in the McGee series up to this point—a dense and tricky tangle of plot and character. That's not to say there aren't serious spasms of violence and a high body count. The narrator makes numerous philosophical digressions throughout the story, as well, commenting upon all manner of mid-'60s issues. By this time, JDM has become more confident that his readers will hang in there as his rangy hero ruminates. The future sidekick—the hairy, semi-retired economist Meyer—puts in only a few brief appearances. JDM hasn't yet concluded that Travis needs someone to round off his hard edges, someone to be his sounding board and boon companion throughout a storyline.

The tale starts with McGee enjoying one of his periodic bouts of retirement. An old friend named Sam Taggart phones after an absence of three years, with a recovery project in mind. During the conversation, McGee delicately suggests the possibility of Taggart getting in touch with the woman he jilted when he lit out. McGee contacts Nora Gardino, owner of a deluxe women's clothing store. She's thrilled and not a little anxious at the prospect of seeing the man who, if things had been different, might have become her husband.

When the two men meet, Taggart tells Travis about the little Mexican fishing village he'd lived in, Puerto Altamara, where he had acquired and lost a fortune. It seems he came into a collection of twenty-eight pre-Columbian gold figurines worth $300,000 or more (several million in today's dollars). He won't share the details. All but one had been taken away from him and he knows that McGee is in the business of restoring lost property, among other things. But with the prospect of seeing his old fiancée—maybe even taking up with her again—Taggart gives up on the notion of reclaiming his stolen figurines. He decides to sell the last one. A man is coming soon to pick it up and pay out over twelve grand.

Nora and Travis drive to the fleabag motel Taggart is staying at. When he gets out, Travis insists Nora stay in Miss Agnes, his Rolls Royce pickup truck.

Personal digression here: Miss Agnes is one of two serial affectations that JDM adopted for the McGee series that drive me up the wall. That someone like McGee, who relies on relative anonymity for his livelihood and personal security, should drive such a flamboyant and ridiculous vehicle strains credulity. It's pure self-indulgence on JDM's part and rings like a sour note in a piano sonata. Would McGee have driven around in a clown car with bells clanging and lights flashing?

Why couldn't it have been a beloved old Ford or Chev pickup? JDM's other annoying tic is the proclivity of almost every female whom McGee knows for more than a few minutes to call him "Darling." I don't buy that either. It's the primary reason my wife isn't all that fond of these books—another false and clangorous note. Rant concluded, and back to Travis and Nora at the motel.

The moment McGee walks into Taggart's room, a sharp metallic smell assaults his nostrils—coppery and pungent. The smell of copious fresh blood. His friend is lying in a sea of red, throat slashed. A little too late, McGee hears tidy footsteps on the cinder walk behind him. Nora sees her old lover before Travis can stop her. Naturally, white knight McGee cares for the hysterical lady.

When the dust settles, the fiery Nora—so close to getting her man and her dream back—demands vengeance. And McGee, of course, is just the one to provide it. They need to find out more about the figurines and who might have been involved with them. First stop is an archeology professor, who educates McGee on these types of objects and provides the name of a Manhattan gallery that would know the market. At the gallery, McGee, operating under the false flag of "Sam Taggart," hints that he might be in possession of twenty-eight figurines. And would they be interested in them? One of the gallery owners shows McGee some photos and among them he spies the figurine that Taggart had. Through various bits of chicanery—including bedding one of the gallery owners—McGee identifies his target: A Cuban exile named Carlos Menterez, who had bought some of figurines from the gallery. A Cuban friend tells him that Menterez was a crony of the murderous old dictator Batista. Then it's time for McGee and Nora to head down to Puerto Altamara, Sam Taggart's last known abode.

South of the border, McGee learns quickly that Taggart had worked as a charter boat captain and was not much missed. McGee connects with a young hooker who was Taggart's girlfriend until he moved into the big, guarded house of one Senor Garcia. She fills him in. After a time ol' Sam took up with the American blonde who lived in Garcia's house. But some kind of trouble happened up there on the hill and Sam had to escape.

At the house, McGee gets Nora to shout "Buenos dias!" to a guard behind the gate. The man answers with a Cuban accent, and McGee begins to zero in on "Senor Garcia."

McGee stages a middle-of-the-night reconnaissance on the Garcia compound. Along the way, he spies someone called Carlos, lying in a bed, totally crippled and dumb from a major stroke. It's Menterez. It so happens that a young American woman is working for the Cuban gangster. By means of a note from Nora hinting at a common interest in one "ST," the couple manages to lure the woman out of Menterez's compound, then hijack her to a spot out in the jungle. Travis ties her to a tree, dismisses Nora, and goes to work.

Almah Hichin, Taggart's blonde, eventually spills the information that McGee and Nora need, without recourse to actual torture. A rich American had lusted for Menterez's collection of pre-Columbian figurines, but Menterez refused to sell. The American sent one of Menterez's old enemies down to intimidate him and later attempt to kill him. Almah and Menterez recruited Taggart and another thug to murder Menterez's enemy and crew. Only when Taggart and the other thug get onto their adversaries' boat, do they discover there's also a woman there—who needs murdering as well, being the only witness. Having killed this innocent woman, Taggart made himself a target for revenge. When Menterez refused to pay Taggart for the crime, Taggart purloined the figurines and headed for the hills.

From this point onward, *A Deadly Shade of Gold* explodes with retribution and violence—as JDM slashes away at the almost-Gordian knot of a plot he's constructed, by way of deconstruction. Taggart, an ostensible good guy, turned out to have been not so good and met the ending he'd earned. Everyone else who deserves death gets it, as well, from Taggart's fellow murderer to the rich American who set the whole bloody mess in motion. But one of the good guys, who doesn't deserve to die, does, if inadvertently. The body count eventually goes north of a dozen. McGee ends up with a nearly fatal gunshot wound himself, after a particularly brutal and incendiary night in a Los Angeles mansion. No one gets out of this story unscathed. (Except Meyer, who didn't have much to do with it in the first place.)

Reading *Gold* is rather like groping through a jungle maze—dark, sodden, rent by unseen screeching and roaring. Bullets whiz by and mantraps open up beneath the feet, with many confusing and scary turnings in all different directions.

I confess that *Gold* isn't one of my favorite McGees, because unlike its four predecessors, it contains its share of wasted motion. It's simply not as lean, propulsive, and compelling—which I take as the highest virtues for mystery and suspense novels. Nevertheless, this tough slog from unrequited revenge to horrified enlightenment is a must for any JDM fan. For a more casual reader—who may not care to read all twenty-one adventures, in or out of order—there are other McGee yarns that would take precedence.

6. Bright Orange for the Shroud

The sixth book in the McGee series is one of the stronger entries—fast-moving and elemental. Travis's mission is to recover the quarter-million (and not a little of the personal dignity) brutally taken from an acquaintance of his. *Bright Orange for the Shroud* (1965) reinforces my view that McGee is at his best when he doesn't stray too far from his moorings at Bahia Mar in Ft. Lauderdale. As entertaining and readable as his out-of-state wanderings can be—I'm thinking *Purple*, *Red*, and *Yellow* in particular—his adventures tramping about the swamps and bikinied-girl beaches and corrupt property developments of Florida are by far the truest and richest expressions of what our knight in dented, tarnished armor is really about.

It's sometime in the mid-'60s. McGee is working on the *Busted Flush*, his big old barge of a houseboat. He's planning on having himself what he calls a "slob summer"—a season of indolence, partying, and cruising among the islands. He hears someone calling his name. At first he doesn't recognize the skinny, feeble-looking man. He realizes it's Arthur Wilkinson, who used to hang out on the margins of Travis's bunch. Arthur's been transformed into a desiccated, sickly stick of a man. He promptly collapses and McGee—not entirely enthusiastically—takes him in. Arthur's old girlfriend was Chookie McCall. (Chookie was the second character to ever appear in a McGee story and the first woman. Remember the dancer at the very beginning of *Blue*? That's Chookie.) Arthur had dumped her for a petite blonde bombshell and Chookie is understandably disinclined to nurse him back to health. But McGee persuades her to look in on poor, malnourished Arthur and the mothering reflex kicks in.

It turns out the instrument of Arthur's near-destruction was the blonde bombshell. Wilma Ferners Wilkinson had the frightening capacity to activate that *zing-zing-zing* reflex of nearly any heterosexual male who crossed her path. He whom she put in her crosshairs was in for a very wild ride and a very hard crash. (Even the vaunted Alabama Tiger, he of the notorious perpetual floating house party, fell afoul of her charms.) The women in Travis's circle—more perceptive than the men, of course—could smell "predator" all over Wilma. She was a scorpion disguised as a june bug.

After she married Arthur, Wilma had herded him away from his friends in Lauderdale and the two moved to Florida's Gulf Coast. She started burning through his small fortune at a ferocious rate and urged him to buy options in a land development that was "very exclusive." *We can quadruple our money*, she gushes. And without lotsa money, how can his sweet little Wilma continue to be happy? Arthur courted the "developers" and they were "persuaded" to let him in. (Sound familiar? It's the Bernie Madoff "exclusivity" gambit.) Arthur signs a dense, barely legal multi-page contract, which requires him to pony up money several more times, basically stripping him down to his skivvies. On his return from a trip, he discovers that his wife has vamoosed, just like his money. After finding her shacked up with one of the "developers," rough ol' Boone "Boo" Waxwell, Arthur realizes how comprehensively he's been conned. Boo beats the bejesus out of him and Arthur spends some months wandering in the wilderness, before turning up at McGee's gangplank.

McGee's plan is to con the con artists. He, Arthur, and Chookie take the *Flush* over to Florida's west coast, where Wilma et al. were last operating. He cozies up to the faux developers' lawyer, gently hauling the bait of an even grander con past the shyster's eager nose. Then he goes after Boo—JDM's nastiest piece of work since *Blue*'s Junior Allen. His intention is to entice Boo into the reverse con. But by the time Travis is finished with him, including one of JDM's niftiest dustups, he has a queasy feeling that the wily, muscular, violent swamp-dweller is nothing to trifle with.

Moreover, while visiting Boo's place, the knockabout knight errant notices lots of expensive toys that Boo couldn't have afforded on his own cut of the

Wilkinson con. Travis's conclusion: Boo used, then killed Wilma and tucked her away in the Everglades mud, appropriating her loot and that of another grifter. The trick will be luring him away from his lair, so that Travis can find the money. Help with that might come from another quarter—from the lawyer's wife, in whom Boo has shown unwholesome interest. But Boo is two steps ahead of Travis. Naturally, all bloody hell breaks loose.

Travis doesn't quite dodge a bullet. The lawyer and his wife have a very, *very* bad evening indeed. Arthur is obliged to call upon reserves of courage he didn't know he had. Travis makes sure that the law develops a profound interest in putting ol' Boo out of commission. A decent portion of Arthur's money is redeemed. And it seems that Travis, Chookie, and Arthur have earned a happy ending.

But as is often the case in the closing acts of these adventures, the Grendel of the moment lurches out of the shadows for one more go at McGee's Beowulf. And with a little help from Chookie and Mother Nature, the monster takes his final bow.

Orange is a dramatic change from its immediate predecessor, the somewhat prolix and overwrought *A Deadly Shade of Gold*. It's lean. It's mean. It's as slick as snot on a doorknob and compelling as a punch in the gut. JDM wastes few motions and his editorializing via Travis isn't overdone.

While there are other Florida-set McGees I enjoy more, *Orange* does proud to the series. If you're a McGee neophyte and *Orange* should cross your path, don't hesitate. Pick it up and spend some time with Travis, Chookie, and ol' Boo.

7. Darker than Amber

Travis McGee and his best friend Meyer are innocently fishing for snook late at night, beneath a bridge in the Florida Keys. Above them, there's a squeal of tires and suddenly a very surprising package comes hurtling down into the inky black water—a woman, bound and wired up to a cement block. Reflexively, the knight in tarnished armor tosses aside his tackle and dives in. He manages to find her in the submarine darkness but has a hell of a time detaching her from the cement block. He needs air. But he knows that if he goes back up for a breath, she'll truly sleep with the fishes. With a nearly superhuman effort, McGee untangles the wire and hauls the semi-conscious victim back up to the surface.

McGee and Meyer bring her back to the *Busted Flush* for recuperation. It turns out she's a hooker by the name of Vangie (short for Evangeline), who's been involved with a group of homicidal grifters. Their stock-in-trade is targeting single, middle-aged men of minor means—enough to be worth targeting, but not enough to motivate heirs and cops and squadrons of attorneys. With her not insubstantial charms, Vangie and others like her lure the men off on Caribbean cruises, and set them up for a strong Mickey Finn and an eternal voyage in the briny deep. And nobody much misses them. Vangie felt sorry for one of the targets and tipped him off, sealing her own fate. The exotically lovely and part-Hawaiian Vangie attempts to get in McGee's boxer shorts, but Travis understands how toxic this young woman is. Thus rejected, but thankful for her salvation, she heads out into the night to recover the nest egg she left behind.

Naturally, things don't turn out well for pretty little Vangie, back in the snake pit where she hid her loot. A news report turns up about a woman fitting her description who was smashed nearly to bits by a hit-and-run driver. So violently, in fact, that her body was thrown up and off the second story of a nearby building. Travis views the body—identifiable most especially by a very beautiful eye that was "darker than amber." Motivated by the peculiarly McGee-ian thirst for retribution and treasure, our hero sallies forth with Meyer. Starting with random clues left behind by Vangie, he manages to find her hoard of folding money. But one of her former colleagues—a quick, brutal muscleman called Griff—is on watch. He cuts Travis's escape short, and hauls him out onto a remote area of beach for extermination and burial. But Griff gets sloppy and misses the little "airweight" revolver that Travis has secreted away. And before you can say "hey presto," it's Griff who's lying facedown in a shallow grave in the sand.

Now McGee and Meyer set to work to bring down the whole repulsive enterprise. They figure out which steamer line the murder team operates on, then book themselves onto the final voyage of the season—joining the ship in mid-cruise. Getting it all set up is a complicated scheme. But from the moment Travis cuts off the murder team's bimbo from her killer/partner—positioning himself as her new "protector" and future lover—it goes pretty much like clockwork. He gets her to write a full confession, while promising her a great new career with him. He relieves her partner of all his money, after a sharp, nasty struggle. An actress who's a dead ringer for Vangie awaits the ship at the dock—and utterly freaks out the killer, who's sure that she's dead. The killer goes on a rampage and very nearly gets to the actress playing the defunct hooker. But not quite. Finally, Travis delivers the bimbo to the cops.

Taken purely as a suspense yarn, *Darker than Amber* (1966) is a brisk, tidy, exciting piece of work; not one of the best in the series, but perfectly entertaining. JDM, after all, gives us a fine gang of truly vile villains, first-rate detective work, and a concise, propulsive plotline that carries the reader right along. But the most significant thing about *Amber* isn't JDM's storytelling chops. It's the very important sea change in the series that helps to broaden and enrich the McGee experience: Meyer's promotion from bit player to full-blown co-star.

JDM explicitly understood that after six solo adventures his Don Quixote urgently needed a Sancho Panza.

Travis's pronouncements and observations are the main attraction, of course, but they've become a little too strident and dogmatic. From now on, Meyer becomes the sounding board—and occasional conscience—that a violent (if well-intentioned) man such as McGee needs to not go off the rails. He softens McGee's hard edges.

While virtually every other significant character in the remaining fourteen books is ephemeral—touching McGee for a time, then vanishing into obscurity or death—Meyer remains a constant for our knight in rusty armor, through every manner of triumph and tragedy. Meyer rights McGee's course, when needed. Meyer the professor provides insights into matters social, commercial, and economic. Meyer grounds our hero in everyday decency. The hairy, semi-retired economist listens as only a very, very good friend can.

For my money, Meyer is quite simply *the* Watson of American crime fiction. Short of McGee himself, he's JDM's greatest creation.

8. One Fearful Yellow Eye

One Fearful Yellow Eye takes Travis far, far away from his balmy native habitat—and in early winter, no less. But McGee, of course, will go to any lengths to help a friend. The 1966 novel begins with his descent into Chicago's O'Hare Airport through a wet, chill, gray soup. JDM depicts the airline experience with nearly as much dislike as today's tormented fliers might feel. We forget that, even back then, arcing through the sky in cramped metal tubes was not all that romantic. Meeting him at the gate (do you miss meeting people at the gate as much as I do?) is his friend and former lover, Gloria Doyle Geis.

She had been one of those damaged birdies who washed up on the beaches of Ft. Lauderdale. Her particular wounding had come from the murders of her husband and children. She only failed to take that suicidal walk out into the surf because of malnourishment and exhaustion. McGee had rescued her, revived her, briefly romanced her, built her up, and set her free. Gloria then had the good luck to meet a fine, decent man—Dr. Fortner Geis, a Chicago neurosurgeon some years her senior who was nursing a slow-moving fatal illness. In spite of the doctor's foreshortened time, they married and returned to the Windy City.

In her house on the Lake Michigan shore, amidst the dunes, she tells Travis about her untenable situation. After the doctor died some months earlier, it was discovered that he had been methodically stripping all his investments and bank accounts of their funds. Some equity in the house and a small annuity for Gloria were all that remained. The 600 grand (over $4 million in 2014 dollars) that should have been there was nowhere to be seen. Geis's adult son and daughter think Gloria plundered Daddy's estate—and aren't shy about saying so. The IRS is keeping an eye on her. The young widow admits that having her share of the money would be nice, but money isn't what's important to her. Mostly she wants to discover who put the screws to her husband, and why he felt obliged to pay up. And she wants to clear her own name. The only skeleton she can think of that was rattling around in the good doctor's closet was an unfortunate but understandable fling he had with the housekeeper's buxom daughter, while his beloved first wife was dying. That liaison produced an unexpected baby girl.

Travis dons his gumshoe fedora and gets busy. He interviews the doctor's icy daughter Heidi—a capable but mediocre artist. Then the doctor's long-time OR nurse, who was his lover for a time. Travis talks with the daughter-in-law, who had a better relationship with Geis than her husband did. Next up is the detective who kept an eye on the doctor's illegitimate daughter. Then Travis visits Heidi's ex-hubby, on whom he administers an oddly gratuitous dose of whoop-ass.

Travis learns that a year and a half earlier, certain clear signals had been sent the good doctor's way: The nurse's cat skewered. A grandson kidnapped and quickly released. The daughter's chocolate candy tainted with pepper sauce. A smoke bomb under the hood of Gloria's car. Translation: *Fork over the money or loved ones start to die.* McGee also learns that someone other than the IRS is watching Gloria. These people take McGee down with unsettling ease, though they don't harm him—very, very professional operators. People who speak an unfamiliar foreign language. People to whom he will ultimately be very grateful.

In the midst of Travis's legwork, Gloria, apparently trying to assuage her tattered psyche, takes some acid and goes on a very nasty trip. If the Florida beach bum hadn't found her in the nick of time, *almost literally* baying at the moon, naked on top of a winter sand dune, the lady would have died of exposure. As it is, she survives by a hair's breadth.

By this point, all clues are pointing toward the ex-con husband of the doctor's illegitimate daughter. The daughter has disappeared, possibly murdered. The ex-con has attempted to rape her oldest daughter, and the girl has fled the desolate farmstead where the ex-con had brought her. Things come to a head when that teenager ends up in Chicago with the doctor's older daughter, Heidi. Travis decamps to the farmstead and discovers the dead, gruesomely tortured body of the ex-con and a part of the missing fortune—hidden in a deconstructed Cadillac. Most of the doctor's money has already been removed. The ex-con, by the way, is the owner of the titular "Fearful Yellow Eye."

It seems that this is as far as Travis can take his investigation. Gloria is on the mend. The kids are okay. Travis lures Heidi off to the Caribbean for a few weeks of McGee's Miracle Cure for Frigid Ladies. But certain inconsistencies nag at him. And as he zeroes in on the definitive truth, the ultimate villains are revealed. But the knight in tarnished armor stupidly lumbers into their lair, clanking and shouting "Huzzah," with no real idea of what he's up against—and, doubly stupid, exposes the helpless Heidi to a terrible risk.

McGee, as always, is brutally honest about himself. He knows how close he came to utter disaster—much like that mouse tempting fate with the cobra back in *Pink*.

9. Pale Gray for Guilt

"In all emotional conflicts the thing you find hardest to do is the thing you should do." —Meyer's Law

Pale Gray for Guilt (1968) holds a special place in my heart because it's both the first John D. MacDonald and the first Travis McGee book I ever read.

It was 1989. I'd been taking a mystery-writing course from a novelist named H. Edward Hunsburger. He was a nice guy, a good teacher. I lost touch with him shortly thereafter, and recently learned that he was himself murdered in 2011 in New Mexico—a victim of random street violence.

One time my wife and I had him over for supper. He asked me who my favorite mystery writers were. I mentioned Robert Parker, Ross MacDonald, Dorothy Sayers, and Dashiell Hammett. Ed noted my interest in hard-boiled PI stories and cagily asked, "Ever read John D. MacDonald?" Nope, I said, never heard of him. Ed was appalled—in a joshing way. And he proceeded to tell me that JDM's Travis McGee was the apogee...the summit...the paragon...the best of the best of the first-person crime yarns. And then he told me why. A few weeks later I randomly plucked *Gray* off the shelf at Barnes & Noble. I read it on a trip and was utterly beguiled. Thus began my Travis McGee quest.

Gray remains one of my favorites from among the twenty-one. It has all the elements that compel the Ft. Lauderdale boat bum to bring his best game. It's set close to Slip F-18, in the world of coastal Florida, amidst the machinations of rapacious real estate developers and crooked pols. A good friend—Tush Bannon, who played pro football with Travis—dies horribly in mysterious circumstances. Tush's lovely young widow and kiddies need rescuing.

With McGee in this adventure is Puss Killian, one of the most important women in his entire fictional life. Even though she's keeping important secrets from him—he's not even sure that her name is real—McGee is head over heels for her. McGee's best friend Meyer again plays an important role. Above all, *Gray* casts McGee as the avenging angel. If you like a great first-person crime story, it doesn't get much better than this.

In the early going, Travis connects with Tush at his little marina/motel. The business is dying and relations with his wife Jan are strained. Later, at a chance meeting, Tush tells Travis how the local authorities are trying hard to push him out—to free up his piece of a parcel for some unknown property development. When Travis goes again to the little marina, it's deserted. A phone service man on the site informs him that Tush went and killed "hisself" by dropping an engine block on his own head. Which an unofficial autopsy later shows to have been a miracle of sorts—as Tush seems to have lifted and dropped the engine three times.

Jan had left her husband and didn't know about his death. After McGee and Puss find her, and let her vent her grief, they begin probing the power structure of Shawana County. Jan legally reclaims the marina property the bad guys thought they had possession of. Then she promptly sells it to Travis. As Jan and Travis's attorney observes, it's like they rammed a stick into a big old hornet's nest. Next Travis rams the stick in a little deeper by making a rich offer to another landowner with a larger piece of land. Meyer (the economist) is recruited to design and set up a con for the guy at the top of the swindlers' food chain, a wheeler-dealer named Santo. And the main local operator, Preston LaFrance, is drawn out of his cover. LaFrance, however, seems honestly distraught that Bannon went and smashed himself to jelly.

At this juncture, McGee sustains a kick in the gut. He wakes up one morning to find that Puss has vamoosed, leaving only a sad, affectionate note and a warning that he won't be able to trace her. Travis is utterly deflated and baffled. But for now there's still vengeance to be exacted.

McGee hooks Santo with Meyer's stock scam, involving an obscure equity that seems foolproof but is in fact rotten. Simultaneously McGee sets up Preston

LaFrance with a parallel scam that works a treat. When the conned businessman appears at the *Busted Flush*, spitting and fuming, McGee has the pleasure of explaining why he's relieved him of a hundred grand—payback for Tush Bannon. LaFrance is mystified: Bannon was a nobody, a nonentity waiting to be run over. Santo gets a similar slap in the face—literal as well as figurative. Travis does his best to put the oily operator on the slippery slope to financial failure.

While Meyer clearly has the makings of a great con artist (as McGee observed in *Amber*), the whole operation takes him to places he's not accustomed to, not comfortable with. In an uncharacteristic outburst Meyer suggests a solution to LaFrance for his situation: Suicide.

After the man has left, Meyer expresses surprise at his newfound capacity for vitriol, and he is ashamed. Even as Meyer sticks with McGee for nearly another eighteen years, there will be yet darker places he's taken by this friendship. And readers will puzzle over JDM's ruthless treatment of the semi-retired economist in one of the later adventures.

But all of this, of course, begs the question: *Who killed Tush Bannon and why?* The murder was not really necessary. In typical fashion, JDM brings the accidental killer charging out of the shadows, nearly taking out McGee and the widow Jan. Once again, proximity to Travis proves a very dangerous thing for one of the story's innocents. But, of course, the boat bum's ingenuity and grit save the day. With a huge assist from the lady.

And what about Puss? Why did she ditch McGee?

Near the end of the novel, a letter arrives from the lady, explaining her decision. Six months earlier the neurosurgeon had taken a tumor out of her brain, the bad kind—a death sentence. And it was time for her to return to her husband. She tells Travis not to brood, to live his life full on. *Find yourself another girl*, Puss writes. *And when you're spooning around her late at night, pretend that she's me.*

Puss's elegy cuts deep into Travis's thick, scarred-up hide. She doesn't want him with her in her hour of darkest despair, because he is not entirely solid, not entirely reliable—as her husband is. That at least is how she perceives it. It is a haunting, bittersweet moment, and one of the few places in the entire chronicle where Travis is raw and open and in pain. Here you are apt to ask: Is his dream lifestyle really worth it? One is even tempted to shed a tear for McGee.

At the outset Travis ruminates over Jan Bannon's dislike of him and imagines what she would say: *You don't live a real life, with a wife and family. You evade responsibility. All that matters to you is floating around, having fun.*

McGee in his heyday was the subject of envy for millions of male readers. I mean, no wife? No boss? A parade of attractive, bikinied young ladies? Taking your retirement in installments? Living on a houseboat on the sunny, beautiful east Florida coast? Charging to the rescue time and again? What's not to love? But maybe in *Gray* JDM is simply making a morality tale of the aspects of McGee that Jan Bannon found wanting: *This is not real! This kind of life—even if you pull it off—comes with big costs.*

One final note: Puss Killian is not quite done with Travis McGee. But I'm not going to tell you when or where or why or how. You deserve to have the pleasure of discovering that on your own.

10. The Girl in the Plain Brown Wrapper

The tenth Travis McGee adventure, *The Girl in the Plain Brown Wrapper* (1968), finds him going to bat for a recently deceased friend. Helena Pearson Trescott's first husband had been murdered aboard his boat in the early 1960s, not far from where McGee moored the *Busted Flush*, at Bahia Mar marina in Ft. Lauderdale. He helped the widow and her two daughters in the days after the murder. Later he briefly became Helena's lover on a sailboat cruise. (Though it's now politically incorrect, this was standard procedure for McGee—as a sexual healer of emotionally and physically wounded ladies.)

Flash forward several years. Cancer has taken the lady. McGee arrives back from a salvage expedition to find a letter from her attorney, which contains a check and a note from Helena herself, written just days before her death. Her older daughter, it seems, has suffered some kind of terrible mental breakdown after a miscarriage. Her memory is gone. She's become childlike. She's suicidal, self-destructive. Her husband and kid sister care for her around the clock. Things don't smell right to the dying woman. She asks her old friend and lover—who she knows deals with mysterious circumstances as a "salvage consultant"—to pay a visit and check things out. As a last and very personal favor.

Under the guise of tracking down Helena's old boat, McGee journeys to the Florida town where she died and where her sick daughter Maureen lives with her husband, Tom Pike. Tom's a property developer and big man around town. Bit by bit McGee's antennae begin to quiver at all that's going down.

Maureen's symptoms have baffled all the experts. She's attempted suicide several times by different means, which is very unusual. The doctor who'd been treating her has unaccountably committed suicide himself. The doctor's ex-nurse and boyfriend attempt to intimidate McGee, but of course fail. They're on a campaign to investigate the doctor's death and prove he didn't kill himself. McGee, naturally, ends up sleeping with the attractive young nurse. Who herself is murdered the next day. Pike is having an affair with a neighbor woman. A lot of people have a lot of money tied up in Pike's projects. A political bully boy and agent provocateur is ranging through the landscape, somehow involved. McGee himself is suspected of killing the nurse.

McGee does here what he does so well in his many adventures: He prods and pokes at other characters, as well as the local power structures. He pressurizes the situation so that unknown individuals begin to push back, sometimes in dangerous ways, revealing that there's more here than meets the eye. It's not hard to figure out the villain's identity. Not because the gears and wheels are all that visible, but because of who would logically want to put the demented woman out of action for good.

The convoluted plot doesn't clarify until the end. When revealed, the mechanisms the bad guys relied on to achieve their ends seem rather complicated and improbable. Even for McGee, some ruminations overstay their welcome. One long paean to the mechanics of sexual intercourse, for example, rather takes the joy—not to mention the emotion—out of this usually enjoyable activity. (The passage is not explicit, just dreary and depressing and overwrought.)

Nevertheless, the main point of reading a McGee story is not the plot. It's to spend some hours inside the head of that rangy boat bum and knight errant who quite a few millions of male readers earnestly wished they could have been. (Female readers of McGee, it's been said, wished they could be *with* him.) *Brown* is one of the weaker books in the series, but any McGee fancier will of course want to read it.

As with any McGee, the title is no mere metaphor. *The Girl in the Plain Brown Wrapper* becomes literal in the course of the action—a queasy, unpleasant image that ranks with titles such as *The Long Lavender Look* and *One Fearful Yellow Eye.*

11. Dress Her in Indigo

Dress Her in Indigo (1969) represents the halfway point of the Travis McGee adventures. Eleven down, ten to go.

This time around, McGee is enlisted by his brainiac sidekick, the semi-retired economist known only as Meyer. It seems a banker friend of Meyer's has lost his only child, a daughter, down Mexico way. Lost—as in, deceased, defunct, dead. The young woman had fled south of the border with a group of hippies. The girl accidentally drove herself over the edge of a treacherous mountain road. Ailing old dad doesn't suspect anything untoward, but merely wants to know how his little girl—for whom he never seemed to have enough time when she was alive—spent her final months. Quite simply: Was she happy?

Travis and Meyer fly down to Oaxaca to answer this question. They begin to root around the hippie expatriate community. Some of the kids knew Bix Bowie, but didn't know her well. The group of young people who came south with her—largely on her dime—had a shadowy reputation. They may have dabbled in drug trafficking.

One of them, Rocko, was a dangerous sort—hardly a flower child at all. In fact, a kind of predator of hippies.

Travis and Meyer connect with the retired American theater designer whose car Bix drove over that mountain cliff. Under duress, he reveals what he knows about Bix and about his own ominous dealings with Rocko. Travis gets more than he bargained for from another source of intelligence—a well-preserved member of the lesser British nobility who is an avid, rapacious nymphomaniac.

(Apologies to modern sensibilities here, but JDM did his share of pandering to 1960s chauvinism. This stuff was still in the air then. He was, to his credit, more enlightened than many of his fellow pulp novelists of that era. He was no misogynist, à la Richard Prather and Mickey Spillane. It took Robert Parker's Spenser to make the first significant move away from that outlook—a monogamous gumshoe, no less, loyal for 35 years to the maddeningly ideal Susan Silverman.)

During their sojourn, Travis and Meyer repeatedly bump into an American father searching for his missing daughter. And there's the wealthy, mysterious Frenchwoman with whom Bix stayed in her final days.

As the two Floridians peel back the layers of Bix's life in Oaxaca, the facts of the case become more and more sordid and depressing. The group was indeed into the drug trade, attempting to smuggle heroin into the States. The precious Bix had become a helpless, filthy druggie, prematurely aged. Passed around among the men of the group as an item of sexual utility. Sold to Mexican field workers for a few pesos a time. Surviving members of the nasty little tribe are brutally murdered—presumably at the hand of Rocko. The presumptive villain of the piece stays frustratingly out of reach for much of the story.

To take this account very much further would spoil the surprises. But I think I can start to make certain generalizations about *Indigo* that won't ruin the story for those who read it. And it's time to start expressing my opinions.

What the book clearly intends to do is depict what JDM—a member of the parent generation of the late '60s—believes is a decadent and dangerous youth movement. He does not like hippies, not one little bit. He is very keen indeed to show the dark side of the lifestyle, through his mouthpiece Travis.

This is a "big daddy" figure expressing his extreme disapprobation: *Nothing good can come from this.* Not every hippie depicted in *Indigo* is a depraved druggie, but even the best of them are painted as fools who are playing with fire.

In a sense, this is JDM at his most judgmental. And that is very judgmental indeed: *See what happens to you if you mess with these drugs and disconnect from normal culture?* You end up a burned-out, brutalized addict who drives off a mountain road in Mexico.

And, it turns out, JDM/McGee very much hates something else in *Indigo*. Something JDM/McGee has hated before. It too is another visceral loathing of the 1960s big daddy.

I well understand that every McGee yarn is about somehow making things right vis-à-vis the victim(s). It is about people, innocent or not, who are in extremis or have been murdered. Events and situations are necessarily unnaturally grim, in each and every story. Otherwise, why read them? Most of literature has jeopardy and doom at its core.

But in *Indigo*—one of the most dismal tales in the McGee canon—I think JDM goes over the top. I think it's the work of a very cranky, middle-aged man who's pissed off at the freedom and political contrariness of his son's generation. It's the reflexive detestation of late-1960s political protesters that I saw in my own father, a veteran of the Pacific war. He was an Army medic on Peleliu.

It galled my dad that vast numbers of teenagers and young adults were questioning what the U.S. government was disastrously undertaking in Vietnam. Beyond politics, the long hair galled him. The dope galled him. The weird clothes galled him. The music galled him. The lack of respect galled him. Just as I imagine it all galled JDM.

Despite some worthy McGee perquisites, I don't know if I'll ever return to *Indigo*. My three readings may be enough.

I have to remind myself, though, to put *Indigo* in perspective. It's one of three books out of a series of twenty-one that I don't care for. Pretty good batting average, I'd say.

12. The Long Lavender Look

The Long Lavender Look (1970) finds our hero and his sidekick Meyer on their home turf in Florida. But instead of dark doings unfolding in the environs of Ft. Lauderdale and Miami, this yarn takes place in the backwater of Cypress County.

McGee and Meyer are cruising home from a wedding they've attended, in Travis's Rolls Royce "pickup," Miss Agnes. It's late at night on a two-lane road that bisects swamp and scrubland. In the blink of an eye, a scantily clad young woman darts out onto the road into the headlights. McGee slams the brakes and misses the dark-haired nymph by mere inches, then struggles to get the big Rolls back under control. He very nearly succeeds, but a tire blows and suddenly the two men find themselves upside down in a drainage canal, under water. Meyer hauls McGee out of the vehicle. Within minutes—as they hike back to the nearest outpost of "civilization"—some cracker drives by and takes a couple potshots at them. Then the guy comes back and tries to persuade McGee and Meyer to come out for a palaver. But he's calling them "Orville" and "Hutch." And with this fateful case of mistaken identity, *The Long Lavender Look* chugs into gear.

When the two bedraggled, bug-bitten friends turn up at Henry Perris's service station 'round about dawn, the theme of mistaken identity continues—big time. Instead of being greeted as car-wreck victims in need of a recovery and tow, they're detained on behalf of the sheriff of Cypress County on the charge of murder. It seems a local villain named Frank Baither has been brutally murdered, and McGee and Meyer are thought to be his former henchmen in a famous casino robbery. Someone tortured Baither—recently out of the slammer—to find out where he stashed the cash. A scrap of paper with McGee's handwriting is found at the murder scene, sealing the deal, as far as Sheriff Hyzer is concerned. Once in custody, Meyer gets the sap beaten out of him by Deputy Lew Arnstead. Things are looking grim for the two residents of Bahia Mar until an attorney friend of McGee's rides to the rescue. The murder scene evidence? Obviously a plant—something McGee tossed in the trash at the service station.

Meyer is dispatched home for medical treatment, but Sheriff Hyzer requires McGee to stay. At loose ends in Cypress City, the big boat bum begins to nose around. First, he goes after Deputy Arnstead (Meyer's mangler), who is nowhere to be found. Seems the fellow started going bad months ago and may be hooked on speed. McGee touches base with the man's mother and finds his stash of drugs and X-rated Polaroids. A buxom restaurant hostess who had a short and abusive relationship with Arnstead is McGee's next stop. Her name is Betsy Kapp.

In one of the saddest sequences in the entire twenty-one adventures, Travis romances and romps Betsy with unseemly ease, the better to debrief her about Arnstead. He makes a brutal assessment of her earnest, eager romanticism and wannabe bravery—not to her face, but inside his own head. And maybe JDM is being true here. But it never struck me as forcefully in my earlier encounters with *Lavender* that McGee's disparagement of this basically decent woman is not merely heartbreaking but cruel. I'll tell you, McGee can sometimes be an absolute SOB. It's awfully hard to like him here.

After a night of rumpy-bumpy with Betsy in her cozy, frilly little love nest, McGee goes out to his car to discover the second setup of his sojourn in Cypress County: The dead body of Deputy Arnstead, sprawled in the back seat, skull stove in. McGee and Betsy manage to dispose of the stiff. But would-be heroine Betsy stupidly ignores Travis's directions and ventures beyond the safety of his motel room. And so the lady vanishes. That "long lavender look" memorably belongs to her.

As he peels away the layers of history and corruption, McGee discovers how rotten things truly are in Cypress County—despite the apparently virtuous Sheriff Hyzer. Arnstead's collection of nudie Polaroids doesn't depict his personal harem. Instead, it shows his string of semi-pro hookers. It's his sample book.

It turns out there were two other participants in the big casino heist besides Baither, Orville, and Hutch—garage owner Henry Perris and his stepdaughter Lilo. She's a pretty, randy, sinewy, sadistic little sexpot who was Arnstead's enforcer with his whores. It was Lilo who dashed across Miss Agnes's bow on that fateful late-night drive. Remember how that scrap of paper with Travis's scrawl turned up at the murder scene? And Henry Perris, garage owner, was in on the casino heist? Well, now you begin to see the form of the frame-up and the reasons behind the murder of Baither and the vanishment of Orville and Hutch.

The fog especially begins to lift when McGee is "lured" by Lilo to a remote, rundown trailer home out in the woods on the pretext of some hard, sweaty horizontal dancing. Now of course Travis knows this black-hearted slut is about as trustworthy as a rattlesnake, but he plays along anyhow. And what ensues is one of JDM's virtuoso set pieces of violence, bloodshed, and doom—alone worth the price of admission to *Lavender*. After reading about the occurrence at the old trailer, you'll never look at oyster knives the same way again.

One of my top-five fave McGees, *Lavender* may be the closest JDM ever gets to Southern Gothic. Because, after all, rural Florida—especially circa 1970—is in fact the Deep South. This sinister tale could just as well have been set in Mississippi or Alabama or Louisiana. And it would make a brilliant southern noir up on the silver screen.

In *Lavender* JDM spins a tangled tale. And at times the dense skeins of plotting—both visible and invisible—make for a baffling read. But in the end, it all becomes clear. As for McGee, in the closing pages he is taken very near to death's door, but happily survives in order to bestow upon us nine more adventures.

13. A Tan and Sandy Silence

A Tan and Sandy Silence (1971) finds McGee in an odd, somnambulistic mood, and Meyer uncharacteristically peevish. Something in the way of ennui is crawling around under their skins. They're both pondering existential matters. Neither man seems engaged in any kind of professional or personal struggle at this particular moment. But neither seems to like where he is. The carefree life at Bahia Mar—where most of us would love to be—is seeming a bit empty.

McGee is engaged in a relationship with a wealthy British widow who's in the market for a long-term male companion—handy arm candy—as she marches deeper into middle age. There's nothing the least bit wrong with Jillian Brent-Archer. She's attractive, smart, affectionate, great in the sack, owns a terrific sailboat, and wants to spend her money having a good time with McGee—cruising, partying, making love. What's not to like about that? Well, Travis, gnarly knight errant, finds a life at Jilly's beck and call—however kindly and subtle the lady may be—to be oddly queasying. The very good deal that it would be is not a deal he can accede to. He cannot yet think of a life without the bent lance and rusty armor.

Into the midst of this miasma barges the boorish, unwelcome husband of one of McGee's old flames. It seems Mary Broll three months earlier had discovered her husband Harry pretty much in flagrante delicto and skipped town. Harry—knowing his wife's fondness for Travis—figures that Travis will know where to find her. It's not that Harry doesn't have some feelings for the missus, but he mostly needs her signature on an important financial instrument for a property development he's working on. Thing is, Travis has no idea where Mary is. Really and truly. But Harry doesn't believe him. Harry thinks the big boat bum is holding out on him. He pulls a gun and starts shooting. The owner of the *Flush* just barely averts a nasty outcome. It's not clear which depresses Travis more. That this fool of a philanderer would actually pull the trigger. Or that he, Travis McGee, the supposed professional tough guy, didn't handle himself very professionally. He wonders if he's getting soft, if he's losing his edge.

Now McGee needs to know the story. So he and Meyer don their detective hats and trek down to where Mary Broll has gone to ground: A deluxe resort on the island of Grenada. But when Travis makes his way there, he discovers that the woman in the guesthouse occupied by "Mary Broll" is, in fact, *not* Mary Broll. Upon seeing the imposter, Travis compares the moment to finding a malignant tumor. He puts on his scrubs and picks up his scalpel. As soon as he separates "Mary" from her momentary toy boy, he begins operating, to get the story of what really happened.

"Mary" is actually Lisa Dissat, the cookie with whom Harry Broll was found by the real Mary. She and her cousin Paul Dissat had entangled Harry in a sex-and-money scheme that involved the murder of his wife. Because after Paul arranged for her to discover Harry's affair, the real Mary would never have signed the financial document that Harry needed. So she had to be dispensed with. Complicit in her murder, Harry was stuck with Paul and Lisa, come hell or high water.

The plan was that Lisa would play the real Mary's role for some months off in sunny Grenada, be in touch with real Mary's best friend back home to establish "viability," scam the bank, forge the signature on the document, and get the money to Harry. Faux Mary would arrange a bogus swimming fatality for the long-dead real Mary—body vanished, food for fishes. The new widower would find himself taken to the cleaners by the rapacious Paul...and possibly murdered himself, since he knows who killed his wife.

Travis intends merely to rattle the cages of Lisa and Harry, but spare their lives. For the lethal Paul he lays plans for one McGee Retribution Special. But he is indeed a bit slow and complacent—as Meyer feared at the beginning of the story. Sensing another predator circling his prey, Paul ambushes Travis and very nearly finishes the boat bum for good. Miraculously, Travis escapes by sea (one of his niftiest and luckiest getaways ever), but for a time he's damaged goods.

Travis has another close encounter with Paul—this time with Meyer also in jeopardy. And yet again—surprise, surprise—he just barely avoids doom. But for the forced jollity of the very last pages, *Tan* ends in the kind of dour rumination that opened it. Here McGee makes a kind of uneasy peace with who and what he is. He will remain true to himself. For better or worse.

14. The Scarlet Ruse

The Scarlet Ruse (1973) gets under way in the arcane world of high-stakes philately—stamp collecting. In fact, this might just be the most esoteric professional setting in the entire McGee canon. A friend of Meyer's, Hirsh Fedderman, has a stamp shop in Miami. And he has a big problem that he'd like McGee to address.

The old man's primary business is putting together investment-grade stamp collections for individuals looking to diversify their assets. But into this musty little precinct of Eden has come a serpent. Somehow, some way, someone has switched out the better part of a $400,000 investment collection—beautiful, valuable, pristine specimens—for junk and garbage. What's there now is worth only a few tens of thousands. On most occasions there were three people in the bank vault where the switch could have taken place: Fedderman. His assistant, Mary Alice McDermit. And the client, Frank Sprenger. One other time Fedderman's other employee, Jane Lawson, filled in for Mary Alice.

The culprit certainly wasn't the old man. Sprenger

never even touched the stamps or the portfolio they were in. Of course, Mary Alice—a loyal, beloved employee and stamp fanatic—is outraged when McGee even suggests her connivance. The upstanding Jane seems equally unlikely to have committed the theft. But clearly one of the women did it. Which one?

The setup becomes clearer when McGee talks to an old friend with deep ties to Miami mobsters. Sprenger, it turns out, is the guy who makes sure that all the criminal groups in town get their fair share of the action. (Miami, like Vegas, was "neutral" ground for organized-crime families from other cities, and agreements were made between them. At least according to JDM.) It seems, therefore, that Sprenger has arranged to double his money—keeping the very valuable stamps as well as getting restitution from Fedderman for their "loss." McGee has to figure out how the scam went down, and protect the old stamp dealer from financial and physical harm.

Somehow Sprenger catches wind of McGee's interest in his stamp collection and sends two of his guys to try to buy McGee—to hire the big boat bum to investigate on his behalf. They make it clear that should McGee refuse the fee, it will be taken to mean that he's in on the scam. McGee takes the money, but later persuades the dangerous Sprenger to lay off him.

Things take a nastier turn, though, when Jane Lawson turns up murdered. Her death could signify that she had the $400k stamp collection and someone took it from her. Or that she knew who'd done the job and was shut up in order to protect the real malefactor.

As McGee begins to put together the puzzle pieces, he devises a complicated plan—a master ruse—to draw out and trap Sprenger. It involves sending out Meyer (who is a helluva friend to put himself in such jeopardy) to bait the steely gangster. And it sets up a theatrical scene way the hell out by an obscure mangrove island. The *Busted Flush* is to look abandoned; Travis's little runabout, the *Muñequita*, is partly sunk; a faux corpse is arranged in a rubber dinghy with a big red floppy hat on its "head." Travis has everything all planned out, down to a T. That is, until one of Sprenger's sniper rounds shatters the mirror that covers the hidey-hole upon which McGee's whole strategy depends. Things, of course, go down the crapper in a big hurry. And Travis—as he often does—sustains serious damage. He ends up recuperating under the tender ministrations of a dear old friend from his very first adventure—in fact, McGee Client Number 1.

(Haven't you ever wondered, reading a McGee adventure or watching some action hero show, how these fictional heroes can sustain the breakage that they do and keep on heading back for more? I sure do. I'd love to have an ER doc go through the wounds and injuries of McGee and give an assessment: Is the human body really capable of enduring and bouncing back from all the wounds and injuries that McGee sustained?)

JDM shows his hand earlier in this book than usual.

But in the interest of helping you enjoy a little bit of suspense, I've resisted revealing very much. What I find most enjoyable about *Scarlet* is how someone as canny and smart as McGee can still be snowed by a clever operator. It's fascinating to be there later on, in his head, as he analyzes how he made mistaken assumptions and barged off in wrong directions. How he was played like a Stradivarius.

McGee is very bright, very strong, and very lucky, but Superman he ain't. And that's one of the big reasons why we love him.

15. The Turquoise Lament

Take a married couple you know pretty well. Two people whom you have no reason to distrust or disbelieve.

Yet the young wife is convinced that her new husband intends to kill her. Indeed, he allegedly has made one attempt already, but failed to carry it through. He secreted away another woman on the wife's boat. The wife claims she had photographed this woman, but the woman isn't in the snapshots the wife got back from the store. The young wife exhibits signs of paranoia and mental instability—which she readily acknowledges. But she still holds to her assertion that murder is in her future.

The young husband is utterly at a loss to explain his bride's increasingly disturbed behavior. Now alone on her boat, he's devastated, close to tears. He loves her, and would never knowingly harm her. The bimbo she claimed was hidden away on the sailboat/cruiser? Paranoid fantasy. The murder attempt? A simple accident, a potentially tragic tumble overboard into the waves. His wife needs professional help.

Now imagine that you're Travis McGee—knight errant in rusty armor, righter of miscellaneous wrongs—flying into Honolulu to confront just such a baffling situation. That's how JDM opens *The Turquoise Lament* (1973).

The bride, Pidge, is the daughter of an old friend. She's the one who sent out the SOS. Back when McGee knew her late dad, the pretty teenager had a huge crush on Travis. Indeed, one time she stowed away on the *Busted Flush*, planning for a romantic cruise with the strapping salvage consultant. Travis returned her untouched, spitting and fuming, to her old man. But dad—with whom Travis worked a treasure salvage operation—died in a gruesome traffic accident, and Pidge ends up with the not insignificant estate and the sailboat/cruiser. She meets her future husband, good-natured Howie Brindle, and the fairytale proceeds. That is, until it turns into a melodrama.

Amateur shrink McGee debriefs Pidge and manages to wrangle her to the epiphany that her semi-breakdown was not due to a subtle plot against her life, but to her deep dissatisfaction with her groom. The marriage had been a rebound kind of thing for Pidge. Howie, a decent guy, was just not the man for her. The isolated months aboard the boat merely concentrated and distilled her unhappiness into a bitter liquor of near-insanity. Time to tell poor hubby the bad news. *The big D's comin' your way, Howie.*

Before departing Honolulu, McGee—not to his

credit—relents to Pidge's long-held desire to bed him. Then it's back to Lauderdale and an odd, disjointed Christmas season that is not at all jolly. People are dying in accidents, and even McGee's sidekick Meyer keels over after a swim in the ocean. He has a serious viral infection, and spends many days in the hospital—where McGee keeps an eagle eye on him. The hairy economist has a close call, but survives. Into this uneasy time comes the beginning of a suspicion that McGee made a mistake back in Honolulu.

One of the treasure-hunting crew that McGee was a part of with Pidge's pop turns up on the *Busted Flush*. That old comrade is now the proprietor of a top treasure-hunting company, and a fishy-sounding project has come his way. It seems to be based on the treasure-site research of Pidge's dad, a retired professor. That research—potentially worth many millions—was nowhere to be found after the professor's death. Could one of the financial/legal professionals who had helped handle the professor's estate have purloined it? Then waited a decent interval before attempting to utilize it?

Things take an even more ominous turn when McGee learns that Howie Brindle knew one of those lawyers who had helped Pidge. And that another young woman who once had a relationship with Howie has disappeared. And that bimbo whom Pidge had "imagined" and photographed? She was a real girl who apparently was nowhere to be found. Lots of circumstantial evidence, you say. But what nails it are those pictures, which Pidge gave to Travis. The prints had been tampered with—the three showing no girl on the empty deck had come from another roll of film.

McGee follows the trail of theft and fraud that had put the professor's research into evil hands. His detective work, which includes torturing a key villain, uncovers unexplained accidental deaths that had cropped up in the vicinity of Howie when he was a teenager. Good ol' Howie is sure looking like a "bug," a slippery homicidal psychopath with an engaging smile and manner.

At this very moment Pidge and Howie are ferrying her boat across the Pacific to a potential buyer in American Samoa. It didn't take much to imagine how Pidge's husband might finalize the divorce out on the open sea. At last, it's time to decamp to the South Pacific—to see if the new Grendel can be conquered and the princess saved.

While *The Turquoise Lament* has most of the perquisites of a good McGee yarn, it seems to me that its proportions and pacing are off. The second act—as Travis goes sleuthing, uncovering both the bloody history of Howie, as well as the theft of the treasure plans—is overblown and bulky. As if JDM was just having too much fun here, turning over the rocks to see what crawls out. It's a masterful case study of an unorthodox investigation. But it insistently begs the question: What about the girl?

Why isn't McGee booking a ticket to American Samoa sooner rather than later? If this very valuable life is still available for saving, *save it!* You could reasonably argue that the time it takes for Pidge's boat to get there from Hawaii gives Travis plenty of elbow room for his complex investigations. But that's real-world time, and *Turquoise* ought to exist more in emotional time, in which the girl's fate is of preeminent dramatic importance.

After all the gyrations of the second act, I almost feel that poor Pidge is not a real person who is loved, but a MacGuffin that drives McGee's increasingly frenetic machinations. The ending of the book almost supports this theory.

Of course, that's just my opinion. You, the reader, will have to decide whether or not JDM has miscalculated here—both in terms of dramatic structure and pacing. I'd be curious to know what his editor was saying.

Still, caveats and all, there's much to enjoy. Howie's a fine, creepy psychopath, almost up there with JDM's top three villains—Junior Allen, Boo Waxwell, and Desmin Grizzel. Travis's tender care of Meyer through his illness provides an excellent portrait of true friendship. His sleuthing is clever and produces results. And the final set piece—in which good ol' Howie gets his comeuppance (a "come-down-ance," actually)—is deliciously nerve-wracking.

16. The Dreadful Lemon Sky

You're a pretty young thing who is spending some time around Ft. Lauderdale's Bahia Mar marina in the 1970s, and you're in trouble. It's time to bring in the big artillery. So who do you call?

At the opening of *The Dreadful Lemon Sky* (1974) McGee's asleep on the *Busted Flush* and one of his intruder alerts goes "ding." He jumps awake, prepared for action, only to discover a dainty old squeeze of his huddled in front of his door. It's Carrie Milligan, who made a poor choice of husband a few years earlier and is now on her own. She's aged prematurely, showing lots of hard miles. Not drug or alcohol miles, mind you, but simple old tough times. And she's come to McGee because he's one of the few people she feels she can trust. What her exact problem is, she refuses to say. She only has one favor to ask of her old lover: *Take this hundred grand in cash money, keep it safe, and if I should happen not to come back in the next few weeks, get it to my kid sister.* McGee accepts the sizable wad for safekeeping—for a cut of ten grand. He politely declines a bonk, for old times' sake, and offends the lady. But he shelters her for a night. Then she's gone.

Of course, Carrie doesn't return.

Meyer spots the report in the back pages of a newspaper: Young woman, after running out of gas, struck dead by truck on a country road near the coastal town of Bayside. Carrie Milligan. (If you recall, JDM used a similar device back in *Darker than Amber*—a hooker smashed to pulp in a terrible auto "accident.")

Naturally, an occurrence like this fails to fly with our man Travis. Coincidence? Almost certainly bullshit. Besides, the late Carrie paid him ten large and he aims to earn it. He and Meyer fix up the *Flush* for a "road trip," and start putt-putting their way toward Bayside.

When the two men dock the *Flush* at the marina in Bayside, they walk into a festering stew of scandal and mystery and deadly violence.

Soon after their arrival, the marina owner's drunken, pugnacious husband blunders in and assumes that Travis is coming on to his wife. A quick, brief brawl ensues as Travis defends himself and sends drunken hubby to the hospital—where the guy surprisingly dies. (It's murder, actually.) As Travis and Meyer start digging into Carrie's situation in Bayside, the nasty circumstances come bubbling up. Carrie's former place of employment is going broke; one of its owners has apparently vanished with a bundle from the corporate treasury. The theory the survivors have is that Carrie was in on the scam with the owner.

As for the accident, things don't add up. Meyer

discovers that the gas tank of Carrie's car had been tampered with, to drain out gasoline and strand the young woman out on the road. There are clues inconsistent with an accidental stumble out into the deadly traffic lane, such as a purse left in the car. (In the 1970s, at least, what woman would go ambling out in the middle of the night, seeking gasoline, without her purse?) There's also evidence that someone was in the car with her—someone who may have administered a hearty shove between Carrie's shoulder blades.

Carrie Milligan's trail goes deeper and darker yet, when Travis discovers where her big wad of cash actually came from. Carrie, the disappeared boss, and a few others were pot smugglers. Not pros, but successful enough to make some nice walking-around money. Could an outside operator have come in and applied a Darwinian solution to the small-timers?

Travis and Meyer apply the "hidden body" theory of astronomy to the situation. Is there some unknown person or organization whose gravity distorts the orbits of everyone else? The best candidate is a local attorney who pops up at almost every turn, "Ready" Freddy Van Harn—an up-and-coming political figure and rapacious, kinky lady's man.

When one of Carrie's friends appears on the *Flush* one rainy evening, bearing a brown package that she's just received, Travis has little reason to worry as she starts to open it. But then, *KA-BOOM*...

And five days later, McGee wakes up in the

hospital.

(At the danger of repeating myself re. Trav's injuries, I've been thinking about bumps on the head and the neurological fates of old football players. And quite apart from his brief pro football career, poor Travis suffered concussion after concussion in the execution of his duties as a fictional hero. I wonder if JDM ever pondered the notion of a 60- or 70-year-old McGee stuck in a care center somewhere, forgetful and fragile. In the real world, that might indeed be the fate of battered knights in rusted armor.)

Once he's recovered somewhat, rather than doing what any sensible person like you or I would do—call it a day and cruise home to Lauderdale—McGee begins anew with the poking of sticks into hornets' nests. And he's ultimately rewarded with the unmasking of not one, but two malefactors.

On both occasions, the rangy boat bum feels the cold chill of the grim reaper blow by him very closely indeed. One baddie dies grotesquely, horribly, and (ironically) quite inadvertently. The other, the bomber of the *Busted Flush*—having ambushed and murdered an admirable local cop right in front of McGee—has his ankles shot out by our hero. McGee almost pops a cap between the hobbled villain's eyes. But he reconsiders, due to all the trouble and grief that such an action might bring to his discreet lifestyle.

In *Lemon* JDM has crafted one of the top middle-pack McGees. It has byzantine dealings in a small, corrupt Florida town. It has drug money and power-structure money and political influence all sloshing around. It has a gorgeous widow woman falling into the sack with McGee. It has Meyer, with his wit and wisdom and super-hot chili recipe. It has drug running. It has the *Busted Flush* in a semi-starring role—severely damaged in the bombing, then rising heroically from the ashes, so to speak. It has dark, dark violence and hidden emotion. It has a nifty, convoluted plot. And, of course, above all, it has McGee.

Lemon simply has everything you'd want from a first-class crime/suspense novel.

17. The Empty Copper Sea

Hot on the heels of one small-town Florida adventure in *Lemon*, McGee and Meyer embark on another in *The Empty Copper Sea* (1978). This story, like many in the McGee chronicles, is a salvage operation for the hulking boat bum and his brainy buddy. But this time around, instead of seeking to retrieve treasure or justice, or exact retribution, McGee and Meyer set out to re-inflate the broken bubble of reputation.

It seems that an old acquaintance of the two men—a charter fishing captain named Van Harder—has been professionally disgraced and essentially put out of business. On the face of it, it appears that he got himself drunk while piloting a luxury cruiser through dangerous nighttime waters; so drunk that he lost consciousness for an extended period. The boat's owner, Harder's friend, and two young ladies attempted to bring the cruiser safely into port without Harder's help. In the process, the owner, Hub Lawless, managed to fall overboard and vanish into the waves.

Harder is a devout Christian and near-teetotaler. He

had only part of one drink on the bridge of that cruiser. It had quickly made him go fuzzy and unfocussed, and then had knocked him out. As a former heavy drinker, he knew what a hangover was and how it felt. And this drink produced an outcome nothing like that. Moreover, a single drink shouldn't have had such a dramatic effect. In short, he's convinced that Hub Lawless slipped him a Mickey.

Quite simply, the old captain believes that his good name was stolen from him, and he wants it back.

Of course, the only man for the job is McGee. Pretty soon, he and Meyer air-drop into Timber Bay, on the Gulf Coast, where the incident occurred. Meanwhile, Van Harder slowly brings the *Busted Flush* the four hundred miles down and around from Ft. Lauderdale to join them.

Travis and Meyer start operating in Timber Bay under what's essentially a false flag. They have cast themselves as representatives of a property speculator who's interested in Hub Lawless's holdings in the area.

Pretty soon they're worming their ways into locals' confidences—and, of course, making an enemy or two. There's Lawless's widow (or is she not a widow?), selling off all of hubby's fancy toys (custom rifles and fly rods and so on). There's the clingy piano player at the supper club, hell bent on setting her little hooks into Travis. There's the scary-smart sheriff, who (like every lawman in the series) is awfully suspicious of the rangy visitor. There's Lawless's pugnacious, drug-addled former lieutenant, who promptly gets hospitalized after his instant brawl with Travis. There's the pair of bimbos who accompanied Lawless on his ill-fated cruise.

Lawless's number two—who had also been with him that fateful night—has suffered a major mental breakdown and is being tended by his sister, Gretel. (I don't think I'll spoil anything here by noting that Gretel Howard becomes one of McGee's most important and treasured women.) This fellow admits that Lawless drugged Van Harder's drink. In fact, Gretel and her brother are a fount of inside info on how Hub Lawless converted assets into cash and set up his escape to Mexico with his sexy Swedish girlfriend. Apart from a blip or two—a minor heart attack after Hub jumped off the boat—it all seemed to go well for the fugitive businessman. At least according to Gretel's brother.

Hub Lawless had reason to disappear. His property developments had suffered a horrible run of plain bad luck and were in the process of taking down his other enterprises. It's common knowledge around Timber Bay by the time Travis and Meyer arrive. And the best clue that Lawless had ducked and run is a photo taken by a local citizen—depicting a man who looks a lot like Lawless, sitting in a Mexican sidewalk café some weeks after the boating "accident." Clearly, Lawless would have wanted his death to seem accidental, so that his abandoned wife and kids could collect the substantial life insurance policy.

The final act of the drama involves a lot of sleuthing

without much resolving of anything. That has to wait until the true facts of the case finally emerge from their hiding place. Still, any kind of situation that allows for ongoing McGee ruminations is worthy of our attention. Of course, this being a JDM tale, there's a twist or two coming your way.

In the end, McGee is able to reclaim the stolen "property" that Van Harder wanted back: His reputation and his honor. And the strapping boat bum gets a little something for himself, beyond his customary "salvage" fee.

So how does *Copper* rank in the McGee canon? For me, just bellow my top four (*Blue, Gray, Lavender,* and *Silver*). It has the classic elements: There are dark doings in small-town Florida, the big boat bum's bedrock background. Social observation and cracker-barrel philosophizing occur. Meyer makes insights and provides feedback. Good-looking women are bedded. Brutal fights take place. People die violently. Local power structures are dissected. I know I'm getting repetitive here, but these are evergreen aspects of the McGee chronicles—the things that make for a classic McGee tale.

From *Copper* you can see McGee's final adventure, and I'm already starting to feel morose.

18. The Green Ripper

McGee should be a happy man. And at the very outset of *The Green Ripper* (1979) he is.

Because, for one of the relatively rare periods in his career, he is in a monogamous relationship with an exceptional woman—the stalwart, smart, gorgeous Gretel Howard. You'll recall her as the woman whose brother played a key role in the dark doings of McGee's prior adventure, *The Empty Copper Sea*. Gretel, of course, was innocent of any involvement in that conspiracy.

But Gretel—in addition to being the ideal girl for McGee—is feisty and independent and wants nothing to do with becoming a fixture of the *Busted Flush*, McGee's dumpy houseboat. Maybe some day, but not now. She has already been an appendage of her no-good ex and her demented brother. Nix on the appendage bit.

That's why, in *Green*, she's off working and living at an athletic resort/fat farm in the far burbs of the Miami/Lauderdale metroplex. She manages aspects of the operation and teaches kids tennis. She loves the job, but during her last overnight with McGee notes that something shady appears to be going on at work. It seems foreign investors are circling. More ominously, she has had a chance encounter with someone she had seen years before—a member of a radical religious cult, one Brother Titus.

Then the shit starts hitting the fan.

McGee hears from Gretel that one of the resort's owners, last seen driving Brother Titus around, died in a bicycle accident. Presumably a coronary or stroke caused the mishap.

Then Gretel herself takes ill with some terrible refractory infection that the doctors cannot identify. All that she can remember as a possible cause is an insect bite-like lesion. McGee takes up a vigil in the hospital. But Gretel slips into unconsciousness, burning up from the inside. If she even should survive, she would end up a vegetable. Finally, mercifully, her struggle ends.

But the shit is not done flying. Waiting for McGee on the *Flush* immediately after Gretel's memorial service are two dour men in suits. They say they are from an obscure federal agency that is investigating the late Gretel's former employer. Had she told McGee that anything unusual was going on there? Wisely, Travis mentions only that her boss had died in a freak bike accident. The two men thank him and leave.

Meyer, who's been at Travis's side throughout this ordeal, goes sleuthing, and finds out about the agency and the two suits. There is no such outfit in the government, nor any federal employees with the names given.

Futhermore, a supposed agent of the FAA had appeared out at the development, asking after a small blue airplane that landed there—about the time Gretel saw Brother Titus. Another bogus federal agent?

It's Meyer who makes the leap: Gretel and her boss were murdered because they saw Brother Titus. Had any beans been spilled on the *Flush* about Gretel recognizing Brother Titus, our knight in rusty armor would very probably have suffered a fatal accident or illness of his own. A strange encounter with real feds confirms Meyer's epiphany. Gretel's autopsy had revealed that she was poisoned by means of a sophisticated Soviet assassination technique.

Meyer tries to restrain his friend, telling McGee it's unlikely he could ever get his hands on Gretel's killers. But Travis will have none of that and he goes off the grid, heading west—with nothing on his mind but vengeance. He takes on the alias of a man called Tom McGraw, an unemployed commercial fisherman, hunting the dusty California back roads for his fictional runaway daughter, who took off years earlier and joined some religious outfit out in the woods. "Tom" just wants to see her again.

Then he arrives at the compound of the cult whose operative killed Gretel, where—after a brutal initiation—McGee is "recruited." The young people at the camp are undergoing military training for terrorist action. "Tom McGraw" patiently plays the game of building trust, until his hand is forced.

Finally, McGee begins his bloody work, wreaking revenge for Gretel. One by one, the young fanatics go down. Not, of course, without struggle and peril for our hero.

The Green Ripper seems to me an odd duck among Travis's twenty-one adventures. Half of the book takes place on home turf and feels more or less familiar. But much of the rest of it unfolds amongst the starry-eyed, fanatic, would-be mass murderers who are members of the Church of the Apocrypha. For McGee and for us, there has been no deeper immersion in the world of the bad guys in the other twenty novels. *Green* is certainly a compelling read, but it doesn't really seem like it belongs. It feels to me like JDM got up on the wrong side of his bed one day and started writing. The author, of course, places his boat-bum hero up on soapboxes pretty much constantly. But this one is the biggest soapbox of all. And what is delivered is especially hectoring.

Having said that, I think that *Green* is the most cautionary and prescient of all the McGee yarns. Here we have an instructive tale from the early days of the age of terrorism. JDM, however great his disgust, does try to let these terrible people express who they are and why they are planning acts of mass murder and social disruption. The young terrorists who aim to murder innocent hundreds for the good of mankind and at the behest of their religion sound almost reasonable at times. JDM knows how a terrorist cult works.

What I regret most about *Green* is the road not

taken. JDM chose Grand Guignol over the very interesting things that might have transpired with a Gretel Howard who lived. *Green*'s McGee, while bloody and dramatic, becomes not more interesting, but less interesting. I think that the *Green* that JDM wrote is simply misbegotten, wasteful, wrong.

In fact, JDM himself more or less agreed. He's quoted in Hugh Merrill's biography, *The Red Hot Typewriter*: "*Green Ripper* was, in retrospect, a mistake."

Let's face it. McGee and his serial monogamy and his romping of ladies on leisurely cruises has gotten tired. (The coda of *Green* is exactly one of those indolent cruises, and it is not as much fun as it used to be.) A live Gretel might have shaken things up; challenged McGee in ways that he'd never been challenged; forced our favorite boat bum to grow in unaccustomed directions; opened up far more exciting narrative possibilities. Gretel was JDM's last chance to do such a thing (though of course he couldn't have known that).

But, as has been mentioned before, being close to Travis McGee can be a dangerous thing. Gretel has to die because her murder is the vital narrative device in the book JDM decided to write. No murdered Gretel...no powerful explosion of violence and retribution at the hands of McGee...no *Green Ripper*. Gretel was a real person in *Copper*, but here she becomes an object—a lit fuse in a stick of dynamite. It was JDM's call.

I wish it had been otherwise.

19. Free Fall in Crimson

After the orgy of blood and vengeance that is *The Green Ripper*, *Free Fall in Crimson* (1981) begins in a fairly conventional, comfortable manner.

Our knight in rusted armor is at home on the *Busted Flush*, with his Sancho Panza (Meyer) at his side. They're consulting with the heir of a wealthy chemist. The potential client hadn't gotten along with his difficult father, Ellis Esterland. Now he wants to know about the circumstances surrounding his father's death. Dad was robbed and murdered at an isolated Florida rest stop, even as he was dying of cancer. A tragic case, of course, but simple and straightforward. Or was it? Something, the son believes, didn't smell right with the official story. And who better to flush out the truth than ol' Travis?

After rattling around the Florida hinterlands, checking up on the dead chemist's last days and personal connections—including the lady who had been his companion/caretaker toward the end—McGee comes up with a couple of useful clues. Clue 1: Tracks at the site of the murder and a witness account suggest that the killer may have traveled on a heavy motorcycle. Clue 2: The dead man's third and last wife, an actress, was extremely friendly with a film director/auteur who made his name with two low-budget, cinema verité biker movies that utilized real motorcycle gangs.

Naturally, Travis begins to nose around the edges of the biker movement in Florida, to see if anyone in that world knows about the murder of an old man at a remote rest stop. And with a whiff of Hollywood in the air, he goes through channels to track down Lysa Dean. (As you'll recall, the now-over-the-hill movie siren was Travis's client way back in Adventure Number Four—*The Quick Red Fox*. They parted company in a less than amicable manner.) Lysa provides some inside poop on film director Peter Kesner, whose more recent cinematic efforts have not garnered either critical accolades or decent box-office revenue. It seems he's financing his latest film—and possibly his last chance to reboot his career—with the money Esterland's wife inherited.

The money trail that JDM lays down here is a bit convoluted. Esterland had set up his estate to go to his wife in the event that he pre-deceased his daughter. And that indeed was the situation. (The young woman was in a vegetative coma from a bicycle accident.) That spells a motive for murder for a film director boyfriend who needs to finance a flick. At least as far as McGee can see.

Sailing under false Hollywood colors (courtesy of Lysa Dean), Travis makes his way to Peter Kesner's location in Iowa. The director is shooting a kind of existential hot-air ballooning movie with Esterland's actress widow. Here McGee finally meets the biker who appeared in Kesner's early films—the hulking Desmin Grizzel, aka "Dirty Bob." With his inscrutable round face and scraggly beard and slits of eyes, Grizzel is hard to read. But McGee can tell that the biker senses something in McGee that's off—his radar penetrating and probing our knight in rusty armor. Grizzel perhaps detects another very dangerous man encroaching on his territory.

I consider Desmin/Dirty Bob to be a member of a kind of trifecta of evil, an all-star team of malevolence. He's one of Travis's three nastiest nemeses, along with Junior Allen (*Blue*) and Boo Waxwell (*Orange*). Desmin is like some malign force of nature. And taken by himself, he's a superb creation of villain-hood.

Needless to say, with Travis on location in Iowa, the cat's among the pigeons. He insinuates himself among the filmmakers, goes for a scenic balloon ride (he really likes it), helps a bit with the shoot, and finally reveals his inside knowledge of the plot to kill the old man. Kesner doesn't exactly deny that such a thing might have happened, but refuses any personal guilt. Kesner may well have wished out loud that Esterland would drop dead. And Grizzel and his buddy may have simply done the deed as a (wink wink) unrequested favor.

Travis is left in the position of having no proof that would stand up in court, and prepares to report back to Esterland's son. But on the last day of the shoot, the Iowa locals (very much unlike Iowans I have known, including my mother) stage a mass attack on the movie location. It seems that Grizzel and others have been making porno videos with underage farmers' daughters. Travis escapes the mayhem with Kesner in one of the balloons, and plummets 45 feet to the ground just before the balloon crashes into high-tension wires. Kesner doesn't make it.

Even Travis, of course, is not going to plummet that far without some injuries. And he takes time to mend. However, now a very loose cannon is out there.

Having lost his mentor and pal Peter Kesner—and on the run from the law—Desmin Grizzel goes on a rampage of revenge against those he blames. People are killed in Iowa. Lysa Dean is brutally raped and murdered. Then the biker comes for McGee.

When Grizzel boards the *Busted Flush*, he gains entry by means of Meyer—whom he has broken in some terrible way that is not explicated. The very foundation of Meyer is shattered. The cost of being McGee's best friend has never been higher for the hairy old economist. But McGee is ready for the onslaught, with the help of some professional muscle. Even then, putting down his latest Grendel is a close, close thing.

Okay, enough with the book report. Now, IMO.

I have never liked *Crimson*. In fact, it is the one McGee adventure that I will definitely not read again.

So what is it about *Crimson* that gets under my skin?

Like its soul mate and predecessor, *The Green Ripper*, *Crimson* is a brutal, depressing book. And the directing of that brutality onto Meyer and, to a lesser degree, Lysa Dean simply turns me off. For me, it's a deal-killer. I think the story could have been told effectively without these occurrences. What is the point of murdering a nymphomaniac, over-the-hill movie star in the nastiest way possible? I fail to see what's gained by gutting Meyer. Keep in mind, at the beginning of the next book a year later, he is still a shattered man, still hollowed out.

Why not let Lysa Dean enjoy a narrow escape? Why not have Grizzel, in his very good disguise, come aboard the *Flush* without Meyer?

In addition, the whole rabid Iowa mob attack thing is ridiculously over the top—a big miscalculation on JDM's part.

I can only speculate, but I wonder if at this point in his life JDM was—as Meyer was in the hands of Grizzel—beginning to look death, to look utter darkness in the eye. Though I have not yet personally experienced the revocation of my "immortality" in the face of some close call or terrible diagnosis, I can well imagine what it might feel like. And JDM apparently wanted to bring this into McGee's world—not knowing, of course, that he himself only had five or six years left.

That, of course, is the author's prerogative. But I don't have to like it. I don't have to like that JDM, in a manner, went off the McGee reservation with both *Crimson* and *Green*.

JDM admitted that *Green* was a mistake. I think that *Crimson* was, too.

20. Cinnamon Skin

The penultimate McGee adventure, *Cinnamon Skin* (1982), begins with Meyer still in a deep funk, after his emasculation by Desmin Grizzel, many months earlier.

So, to lift his Sancho Panza's spirit, McGee and some friends finagle him a little secret morale boost: An invitation to speak at a conference in Canada. While the semi-retired economist is away, his niece Norma and her groom Evan Lawrence take over the *John Maynard Keynes* for a few days of fishing and sight-seeing. On their final cruise, they are blown up by a powerful bomb. A radical group supposedly from Chile announces that it had targeted Meyer because of his collusion with the Pinochet regime.

Of course, that's not what was really behind the triple murder. Nor was the murder really what it seemed. McGee manages to track down photos of the *Keynes* from moments before the explosion. Yes, Meyer's niece is in the shots, in her tiny bikini. Yes, the hired captain is there on the bridge. But where the new husband should be there's a fellow who does odd jobs around Bahia Mar. No sign of the husband. Might he have been below decks? Maybe. But why, then, was a second hand needed on the vessel? Hubby could have handled the tasks.

The plot thickens when Travis joins Meyer in Houston, where the economist is settling his niece's estate. Her attorney reveals that her not insubstantial nest egg had been mostly cashed out before her death. Husband Evan is looking to be a murderous con man. As McGee and Meyer follow the sparse trail that Evan left, they discover that he may indeed be a "black widower." When the owner of the real estate company that employed him turns gray and retches upon seeing his photo, because the guy murdered his sister—well, our two heroes know what has to be done.

In the midst of all this, McGee's current paramour, hotel manager Annie Renzetti, dumps him. She's about to be given a big promotion and transferred to a much larger resort in Hawaii, and Travis isn't about to transfer with her. Here, once again, JDM depicts the cost of Travis's fantasy life when it encounters someone who lives in the real world. He's understandably wounded, but it seems too late for him to change.

Travis and Meyer put on their detective caps and begin to trace Evan's history, based on scraps of conversation with him back at Bahia Mar. Meyer finds likely candidates for the young Evan in photos in old Texas college yearbooks. (Evan had mentioned living in Texas as a young man.) Then they go looking for someone who had sold cement garden lanterns in Texas a generation ago. (Evan had described selling them door-to-door.) And they find signs of one of Evan's early crimes, as well as one of his early aliases. It seems that a beloved kid sister had vanished with him, never to be seen again.

Finally, the two sleuths hit pay dirt. Evan turns out to have been a kid named Cody Tom Pittler, who grew up in a Texas border town. He has been on the lam ever since he witnessed his father murder his stepmother, with whom Cody was in flagrante delicto at the time. He, in turn, apparently shot his father. This revelation leads to a trip to New York to talk with Cody's sister, who receives occasional care packages of cash from her brother. She leads our guys back to a go-between in Texas. And that woman, albeit very reluctantly, points them to a name and address in Cancun.

Cody/Evan turns out to be living in a compound down there, where he stays for months at a time. He only leaves it for his fishing jaunts and for some long absences out of town—presumably when he's on the hunt for the gold of his next victim. He remains extremely dangerous, having just murdered an old business partner who apparently knew too much. Travis and Meyer collaborate with the partner's devastated fiancée—a woman of Mayan extraction who helps them set up the endgame. She is Barbara Castillo, she of the cinnamon skin.

Now it begins—the hunter becomes the hunted. But as is often the case in McGee adventures, things don't play out as planned. The situation goes to hell and the good guys have to scramble to survive.

After the über-violent outliers of *Green* and *Crimson*, *Cinnamon* definitely takes us back into the mainstream of the McGee saga. It's a tale of revenge and detection—fairly straightforward by the standard of most McGee novels. It's such a workmanlike yarn that it gives no clue McGee's last hurrah is rapidly approaching. And why should there be premonitions of the end? JDM at this point (1982) probably thought that he would be writing McGees for another decade or two.

(A big sigh from yours truly. Think! Another eight or ten adventures. *Emerald* and *Fuchsia*. *Jade* and *Maroon*. *Black* and *Ochre*. *Coral* and *Beige*. *Plum* and *Salmon*. How great would that have been, even if Travis would have had to slow down and acknowledge the weakening of the muscles and reflexes? His wits would have been more than enough.)

I wouldn't put *Cinnamon* in the very top rank of McGee novels. (My faves remain *Gray*, *Silver*, *Blue*, *Lavender*, and *Copper*.) But it's an impeccable, super-solid, page-turning piece of crime fiction that JDM could be proud of; and that any first-time reader can use to launch his/her exploration of the McGee canon.

21. The Lonely Silver Rain

It's a bittersweet thing, starting to read *The Lonely Silver Rain* (1985).

Because we readers know something that JDM didn't realize in creating the twenty-first novel in this peerless series: That this would be the last adventure for our knight in rusty armor.

After *Silver*, no more Grendels for McGee to hunt and defeat. No more wounded ladies to heal. No more rhapsodies and Jeremiads on the slow death of Florida's natural world. No more hair's-breadth escapes. No more parties aboard the *Busted Flush*. No more Boodles (or Plymouth) on the rocks at the end of long tropical days. All that comes after *Silver* is a wordy chat between Travis and Meyer about books and reading—an eccentric epilog that hardly counts. Then, silence.

I can't say I much like the idea of a world without Travis out there somewhere. Getting on in years, but still hunkered down on the *Flush*. Perhaps at some obscure little marina in the Keys or up the west coast. Retired from the salvage business. Reluctantly collecting Social

Security and Medicare—but still available to consult on strategy and tactics. Walking slowly, with two bum knees. Finally settled down with one lady who manages to not get herself murdered, or die of some terrible disease, or wander off out of apathy. We don't know her name, but we would like her. With frequent visits from a now-white-haired Meyer and others who love the old beach bum. I guess that we can dream he's still with us, like Elvis.

As for *Silver*, I wouldn't argue the point if you said it was the best of the twenty-one—and an unintentionally apt conclusion to the McGee epic. (I wouldn't argue if you said the numero uno was *Blue* or *Gray*, either.)

The yarn gets under way in typical McGee style, with an old chum coming to our guy for help with a salvage project. It seems that Billy Ingraham's new, custom, 54-foot cruiser was stolen right out from under his nose—as he and his wife lounged on an isolated Florida beach. It's been gone for months and no one has been able to find it. Would McGee give it a shot?

Travis is a little reluctant at first. Locating a boat like this in Florida is like hunting for a particular grain of sand in the Sahara. But an aerial photo of the cruiser gives him an angle. Seen from above, Ingraham's vessel looks vaguely like an elongated smiley face, a unique configuration. Travis puts an aviator pal on the job, shooting pictures of marinas hither and yon. After peering at thousands of pleasure boats, McGee and Meyer spot the *Sundowner*. It's at a tiny marina on Big

Pine Key.

Of course, by the time McGee gets to where the boat was when it had its picture taken, it's gone. He puts his flyer back in the air, cruising the nearby islands and inlets, in case the *Sundowner* hasn't gone very far. And they hit pay dirt again. She's tucked away in some mangroves just a dozen miles northwest.

When Travis arrives on the scene, it's a horror show. Carrion flies are zooming in and out of the *Sundowner*, and the stench of death is blooming in the hot, muggy air. Inside are the teenaged boy and girl who stole the boat, and another unknown girl. Clearly, they were involved in some kind of drug deal gone horrifically bad. Our hero vamooses out of there and anonymously notifies the Coast Guard. The *Sundowner* is ultimately returned to Billy Ingraham, who claws back some of his costs and pays Travis. But this yarn is far from over.

Someone out there figures out the identity of the anonymous tipster. And sends Travis a little letter bomb—that propitiously explodes elsewhere, to the detriment of some young thieves. Then, soon after, Billy Ingraham dies while on holiday in France. Someone slipped a piano wire in through the corner of his eye. The whodunit is solved, more or less, by his widow—a former paramour of top-level Miami drug dealers. She calls an old lover who knows the coke trade. The key to everything is the second dead girl, who turns out to have been the beloved niece of a Peruvian drug lord. Anyone who had anything to do with the *Sundowner* is now a target for revenge. Travis tries, unsuccessfully, to get a message to the bad guys: *I didn't do anything! I'm innocent.* But it doesn't get through. Another attempt is made, and three would-be assassins learn that ol' Travis is not to be trifled with.

In the midst of all this, someone's messing with McGee's head—leaving strange little gifts for him on the *Flush*. Pipe cleaners twisted into cat shapes. He can't make any sense of them, and he sure doesn't like it.

It takes a trip to the Yucatan with a DEA agent (long story) for Travis to learn who's behind the hit campaign.

The story of the murdered kids is this: The boat thieves carried two loads of coke back from Mexico. The second time, the boy paid the supplier with bogus bills and kept the seventy-five grand that his American boss had given him—thinking himself very clever. His American boss is the son of a major Miami mafioso and responds by killing the boy and his two companions. Ruffino Marino, Jr., had no idea the second girl has Peruvian drug connections. When he finds out, he tags McGee and Billy Ingraham: *Travis and Billy killed the kids as revenge for the boat theft.* Then the young Mafia guy sets hit men on our hero and his client to placate the Peruvians.

McGee manages to get the truth to the people who count, removing himself from the line of fire. And a bloody war breaks out between the old mobsters and the South Americans. In the midst of this chaos, Marino, Jr.—the one the Peruvians *really* want—goes to ground.

With the help of a mafia hit man who's on the run because of the mob war, Travis tracks down Marino and delivers him to a friendly lawman tied in a bow. Actually, Travis glues Marino's hands, thighs, and lips together with super glue. And he makes sure word gets out to the proper people: *Here's where you will find the killer/rapist of the drug lord's niece.*

But the McGee epic is not quite done. There's one more mystery to solve: Who's leaving those pipe-cleaner cats? And why?

For the answer to that, you'll have to read *Silver* yourself. I wouldn't dream of spoiling your fun.

By the very end, Travis's equanimity and optimism have been restored. The *Flush* has chugged up the Waterway, to an anchorage in a quiet bay. The old barge is packed with friends—partying and drinking and talking. Some of them are familiar names from past adventures. Meyer, of course, is present, with cauldrons of his wicked hot chili. Travis's most recent lady is asleep in the sun.

"I study the amount of tan on her smooth broad back and I peer at the angle of the sun and decide she's in no danger of burning," Travis reflects. "In a momentary flash of panic I believe the gaudy boat, the noisy people, everything is dead and gone, imagined long ago and forgotten. It passes."

What JDM gave us was indeed imagined long ago.
But dead? Gone? Forgotten?
Never!

Travis McGee lives forever!

Now where did I put my copy of *The Deep Blue Good-By?*

About the Author

D. R. Martin is the author of the Johnny Graphic middle-grade ghost adventure series, the Marta Hjelm mystery *Smoking Ruin*, and two books of literary commentary: *Travis McGee & Me* and *Four Science Fiction Masters*. Under the pen name Richard Audry, he writes the Mary MacDougall historical mystery series and the King Harald Canine Cozy mystery series.

You can follow D. R. Martin at drmartinbooks.com.

D. R. Martin's Travis McGee & Me blog continues on at https://drmar120.wordpress.com/.

If you have questions or comments, you can contact D. R. at drmartin120@gmail.com.

www.ingramcontent.com/pod-product-compliance
Lightning Source LLC
Chambersburg PA
CBHW031408040426
42444CB00005B/472